Call 2 Ministry

Exploring the Myths, the Mystery, and the Meaning Of Following God's Call Into Vocational Ministry

By Dana Mathewson

Blessings to you!

Dana Mathewson

19/2 10:45

Contact the author at
Call2Ministry
Attn: **Dana Mathewson**
P.O. Box 1215
Seymour, TN 37865

Website: www.ministry4life.com
Email: dana@ministry4life.com
Phone: 865.607.0326

Xulon Press
www.XulonPress.com

Xulon Press books are available in bookstores everywhere, and on the Web at www.XulonPress.com.

Dedication

I dedicate this book first to my mother, Jeanie Mathewson, who dedicated me to the Lord unselfishly while I was a newborn infant. Through all my awkward phases, selfish acts of rebellion, and difficult times, she never stopped believing that God would work in my life. She prayed constantly that I would become the man of God the heavenly Father intended.

I am also eternally grateful to Clete Sipes, a dear friend who showed me how to have a quiet time with Christ Jesus. Clete is an adept disciple maker who spent many hours mentoring me, pouring kingdom principles into my life. Under his leadership, I began my own vocational ministry pilgrimage as a sophomore in college. To God be the glory!

Acknowledgements

I am very grateful to my devoted wife, Jennifer, who spurred me on to fulfill part of a dream that included writing this book. To my sons, Daniel and Micah – may you grow in stature and in wisdom to become the heavenly Father's instruments of grace and glory.

Contents

Foreword

"If God called you to preach," Philips Brooks said, "Don't stoop to be a king." No greater honor can be given to a saint of God than to receive the call to vocational ministry. As a teacher of hundreds of students annually at Southeastern Baptist Seminary, I am reminded daily of the wonder of the call of God as I see it lived out in these chosen vessels.

My relationship with Dana Mathewson goes back to my own seminary days as we worked with a youth group together. His passion for students and desire to see them grow in Christ has continued from then until now, prompting him to write this helpful book on God's call to vocational ministry. You will find this book filled with practical, biblical, and needful information for those wondering whether God may be calling them to Christian ministry.

As I have preached in many hundreds of churches over the years, it seems that the challenge to young people to consider whether God may be calling them to the ministry has waned. In a society where both morally and spiritually the culture seems headed down the sewer, more than ever we must challenge students to consider the call. And, as we extend the call, we now have a handy reference to give to anyone seeking to discern the mind of God for their own life in this matter.

The U.S. Census Bureau tells us that in the years following 2006 we will have more youth in the United States than at any time in our history. Pray that God will call many of these to a radical commitment to serve God in the ministry. And when someone comes to you wondering about the call of God on his or her life, have a copy of *Call2Ministry* ready to give them!

Alvin L. Reid, Ph.D
Professor of Evangelism/Bailey Smith
Chair of Evangelism
Southeastern Baptist Theological Seminary
Wake Forest, North Carolina
August, 2003

Introduction

Have you ever asked a question and received an answer that only confused you? I can sure relate to that. When I was a child, I asked my mother the eternally important, life-altering question that every kid wants to know: "How will I know when I meet the right person to marry?" I waited with great anticipation to hear her say, "You just know." Boy, was I sorry I asked. I was a young man before I came to understand the significance of those words as I gazed, heart-smitten, at the young woman who would become my precious wife. In that moment "I just knew." After nineteen years of marriage, we're even more convinced that we're right for each other. So, my mother's answer, although frustrating at the time, was right.

How did my mother "just know"? What intuitive knowledge did she possess? My mother was a godly woman who loved the Lord Jesus, studied His Word, and enjoyed a wonderful relationship with Him. She didn't have the academic credentials of an expert in relationships – no college or honorary degrees, no knowledge of New Testament Greek. So then what made her words trustworthy? Her unwavering walk with God. When I became an adult, I understood that, but her original answer of "You just know," was frustrating and even discouraging because it had to do with the rest of my life!

You may have picked up this book because you are wrestling with the process of vocational ministry. Something deep in the core of your heart asks, "Is God calling me to something special?" Or perhaps you are certain that God is leading you to vocational Christian service, and you desire a stronger sense of confirmation and direction concerning the next step. You may have heard the same answer of "You just know" from someone you admire and trust, and that answer is confusing you or even causing frustration.

You are not alone in this struggle. As long as God has been intervening in the life of believers, beckoning them to take up His call, frustration, discouragement, and confusion have surfaced. Even the Apostle Paul struggled at the outset of his ministry. He took some time to sort things out in the desert of Arabia. He writes of it in Galatians, "But when He who had set me apart, even from my mother's womb, and called me through His grace, was pleased to reveal His Son in me, that I might preach Him among the Gentiles, I did not immediately consult with flesh and blood, nor did I go up to Jerusalem to those who were apostles before me; but I went away to Arabia, and returned once more to Damascus" (1:15-17). Paul did not discuss his call with anyone at first; instead, he went to a solitary place possibly to pray and sift through his thoughts to clarify the call God had placed in his heart. Maybe you are facing a "desert" experience of your own, trying to discern God's leading for the rest of your life. It is my sincere hope and prayer that as you read this book, the Holy Spirit will speak to your heart with the assuring peace that passes all understanding. "God has a wonderful plan for your life" is an often quoted cliché, but it bears much truth. He wants to confirm His wonderful plan in your heart moving you beyond the point of "You just know," beyond the myths and mystery that seem to surround the call, and on to the true meaning of what He wants to do in and through you.

If your life plan does not include vocational ministry, I pray for you to understand that God can use you for His glory in another career. Thousands of people serve Christ daily as teachers, doctors, engineers, carpenters, and in practically every honest occupation. These people are using their businesses and places of employment to impact the world for Christ, and their contributions to His cause are vital, as yours will be when you walk surrendered to God's will. If after reading this material you realize that God is not leading you into vocational ministry, then I pray He will place an abiding peace in your life to help you understand *your* personal life ministry. However, if the Lord *is* leading you to serve Him vocationally, then this material can give you confidence to prepare for the next step. Whether you are being led into vocational Christian service or not, you have won a major victory by accepting God's marvelous will for your life. Hopefully this book will help you gain more insight into those three little words: "You just know." Beginning each chapter are testimonies written by real people who have heard the call of God to ministry and followed it. As you read of their joys and frustrations, you may find similarities to your own story. May their words comfort and inspire you on the path of the call to ministry.

Part One: Discerning the Call

CHAPTER ONE

If You Can Do Anything Else, Do It!

I *guess, looking back, I knew from my teenage years that God had a special plan for my life. I was the one in the youth group who people always came to for advice. I was the one in the youth group who was always put in charge of leading activities. I was even the "Pastor" of Youth Week my junior and senior years in high school. I remember my youth pastor sitting me down one day, while on a youth mission trip, and telling me he felt God was going to do something special in my life, maybe even call me into the ministry. I think that was one of the best belly laughs I had ever had up to that point in my life. I remember thinking, "Yeah right, you can't be a minister and be cool at the same time. Plus, ministers have to be perfect and everything, and I am far from perfect."*

I graduated high school and went to college, not to necessarily earn a degree, but to play football. Earning a degree was just a by-product of playing football. I decided to be a history major so I could teach high school and coach football. After about two years of acting like a college student, along with having a grade point average in negative figures, the school asked me to take some time off to, "Reevaluate my academic future." I had been kicked out of school! This really threw a monkey wrench into my plans. I was about to get married. I was already doing some coaching for a middle school, and I had already made plans for where we were going to live and even the kind of car I was going to buy when I got my first coaching job. Again, looking back, it's funny to see how "God works all things together for good for those who love Him" (Romans 8:28). I thought, at this point in my life, I had hit bottom and all was lost.

Shortly after this, God allowed me to marry way above my head. He had provided for me the most godly woman in the world. She is beautiful both physically and spiritually. She is the one who kept me grounded and rooted in God's Word. I would hear her praying for me that God would give me direction and that He would reveal His will for my life to me in His time. I must admit, my life at that point had no real direction. In the first two years of our marriage, I had bounced from job to job just to help make ends meet. Her teaching career was taking off, and I was cleaning bed pans at a local hospital. I needed a career. I needed to finish college.

I reenrolled at my former college and listed my major as Physical Education with a minor in Sports Medicine. I had finally found my place, or so I thought. With the few credit hours I was able to retain from my earlier time there, I could graduate in five semesters. I studied hard and learned everything I could. I took all the classes that ended with the suffix "-ology." I was working at a local physical therapy clinic as well as the college athletic training room. I was traveling all over the Southeast with different athletic teams and had even been asked to work at the Amateur Athletic Union Junior Olympics, and to teach some break-out sessions pertaining to Sports Medicine at some local high school coaching clinics. I was on my way! I had it all lined up. **I** *had all the right connections.* **I** *knew all the right people. There was just one problem. The National Athletic Trainers Association has a test that any aspiring athletic trainer must pass before he or she can get a job. It is a beast of a test that covers two days. It's like the bar for lawyers or the boards for doctors. I took the test four times and had passed two of the three parts on the first try. I continued to fail the third, and final, part by less than five points each time. Talk about frustrated and discouraged! How could God not allow* **my** *plans to come together?*

After the fifth attempt at the test with the same results, I felt I was at an even lower point than before. I was married. I had a lovely baby girl. I had a mortgage and car payments. I had a college degree and yet I was working at a juvenile detention center making peanuts. I worked nights. My wife worked days. We hardly saw each other and our relationship was strained, to say the least. But, through all this I was faithful in Bible study. I was teaching Sunday School at my church and becoming as involved as I could there. It was during this "down" time in my life that I began to really cry out to God to show me His will for my life. I was finally begging to understand that my plans may not be His plans for my life. Then one day during my quiet time, it happened. I was reading through Isaiah and I came to Isaiah 55:8, 9; " 'For My thoughts are not your thoughts, Neither are your ways My ways,' declares the LORD. 'For as the heavens are higher than the earth, So are My ways higher than your ways, And My thoughts than your thoughts.'" Now I have never heard God speak to me audibly, but that day I heard Him louder and clearer than ever before. It was then that He revealed to me that all my plans were just that, my plans, and when I compared my plans to those verses of scripture, I realized they were the wrong plans.

Immediately after finishing that quiet time, I called my pastor and asked to speak to him. I told him what I felt God had revealed to me, that He was calling me to full-time vocational ministry, and he confirmed what my youth pastor had told me all those many years ago. My pastor told me that I needed to discuss it with my wife, and if God had revealed the same thing to her, I would have even more confirmation. That evening after dinner, I sat my wife down and told her all about why I felt God was leading me in this direction. With tears streaming down her face, she took my hand, looked me right in the eyes and said, "I've known this for a long time. I've just been waiting for God to get it through your thick head."

That was almost eight years ago. Since that time, God has allowed me to be on staff at some wonderful churches, and He has allowed me to be a small part of seeing lives changes for eternity. It humbles and amazes me every day that, after years of disobedience to His will for my life, He would still allow me to be a minister. Even though I am so unworthy of His blessings and grace, He continues to pour them out upon me every day. Though there are many regrets from my years of disobedience, my greatest regret is in knowing that I missed the blessings of those years when I was following my will and not God's.

—Chris

A number of years ago, a newspaper headline in a major city claimed that a California church possessed one thousand ministers. Most people assumed that one thousand people were serving on the church's staff. But the article explained that one of the purposes of the church was to assist its members in finding their way to serve others. That, in fact, all of its one thousand members are ministers. Often we associate the word *minister* with pastors, evangelists, missionaries, or church staff, yet all Christians have unique temperaments, gifts, and talents which enable them to participate in personal ministry. Whether you believe God is leading you into vocational ministry or not, you must understand that every believer shares a personal ministry.

Because we are all called to minister, we should understand ministry. The word *ministry* comes from the word in the New Testament for 'deacon.' In fact, the word was an everyday part of the Greco-Roman culture before the church was established. In its literal root form, it simply means 'to wait or serve a table.' At its basic meaning, ministry is servanthood, which all believers are equipped to do. Ministry is not set apart for an elite few in the church. You may not be able to sing a melody or teach eloquently from a biblical theme, but God has gifted you to meet the needs of people in other ways.

There are many ways to serve the church body. Although some areas are considered "behind-the-scenes," they are nonetheless critical to the healthy function of the church. For instance, one member of our congregation comes to the church facilities about once a week to check all appliances and bathroom fixtures, makes note of those that need repair, and then repairs them. One precious lady in our church prepares bags filled with goodies and gives them to the elderly people she visits in nursing homes. Another man with mechanical skills changes oil and does light car repair for widows. If I tried to repair a car, it would not be a ministry, it would be a disaster! I am not skilled in car repair, but those who are contribute a great personal ministry for the church body, even though they are not in the limelight. Such "behind-the-scenes" servants do not have seminary training; they do not serve on a church staff; they do not preach, teach, or lead worship. However, at the heart of their labor is service to others for the glory of God. This is true ministry.

Jesus Himself gave us a picture of true service when He said of His own ministry, "For even the Son of Man did not come to be served, but to serve, and to give His life a ransom for many" (Mark 10:45). A Christian's model in ministry should first and primarily be the Lord Jesus. His focus was on serving others, not vice versa; therefore, our focus as believers in Christ is to give of ourselves to minister and to serve. We are not saved to sit around and become saturated in knowledge, to eventually stagnate and be of no use. We are saved to serve the needs of others for an eternal purpose.

When viewed in an eternal perspective, no ministry is insignificant. If the word ministry means 'to wait a table' or 'to attend a need,' then every Christian is able to participate in some ministry capacity that will further the kingdom work of Christ. Ministry in this context is service to other people in Jesus'name. There are two kinds of ministry service: **equipping ministry** and **marketplace ministry**. Most Christians are involved in both kinds of ministry service at one time or another in their lives. Let me explain these ministries:

1. **Equipping ministry** draws people who believe that God has set them apart for the purpose of equipping other Christians for the work of ministry, whether the church is gathered or scattered out in the community. Paul lists some equipping ministers in Ephesians 4:11-13 as he writes, "And He gave some as apostles, and some as prophets, and some as evangelists, and some as pastors and teachers, for the equipping of the saints for the work of service, to the building up of the body of Christ; until we all attain to the unity of the faith, and of the knowledge of the Son of God, to a mature man, to the measure of the stature which belongs to the fullness of Christ." People involved in the ministry of equipping have a passion to teach and edify other

believers for various areas of service in the church and the community. They are local church elders, staff ministers, pastors, Bible teachers and professors, missionaries, and overseers of various ministries which serve and equip people for service. These folks may be bi-vocational or they may serve full-time. The purpose of this book is aimed directly at those who feel God is calling them toward such an equipping ministry.

2. **Marketplace ministry** involves Christians who have chosen a career which enables them to impact others around them for the cause of Christ. Most believers fit into this type of ministry. These people are carpenters, doctors, homemakers, businessmen and women, etc. They are blue collar workers as well as professional people of all occupations. They look for opportunities on the job to share Christ and even disciple believers in the faith. As the Lord gives them greater leadership positions and influence, they are able to impact people in their marketplace area for the glory of God. In Paul's day merchants, doctors, lawyers, fishermen, farmers, politicians, couriers, and others served as marketplace missionaries in strategic places to influence fellow workers, employees, clients, customers, and constituents for the cause of Christ. Marketplace ministers may still lead or serve in some way when the church is gathered, but their primary ministry opportunity is in the community in their particular career marketplace.

Whether in the church, marketplace, or community each of us is called to serve. Paul explains this to the believers in Rome, "Through whom (Jesus) we have received grace and apostleship to bring about the obedience of faith among all Gentiles for His name's sake, among whom you also are the called of Jesus Christ. . ." (Romans 1:5-6). Since all believers are called of Jesus, all are to affect their world for Christ. Paul encourages believers in Ephesus as he writes, "I pray that the eyes of your heart may be enlightened, so that you will know what is the hope of His calling, what are the riches of the glory of His inheritance in the saints, and what is the surpassing greatness of His power toward us who believe" (Ephesians 1:18-19b). He admonishes them to know their hope and their inheritance so they may freely and confidently share with others.

As Paul understood, we are all called to salvation and to service as we mature in the faith. In that respect, every believer is called to some type of ministry. The question is not "Are you called to ministry?" The question is "Are you called to be an equipping minister or a marketplace minister?" Sometimes God calls men and women out of the marketplace and into equipping. Sometimes He calls them out of an equipping ministry and into the marketplace. I know successful businessmen whom God has called to the pastorate or other equipping ministries. I have also known faithful church staff ministers who were led of God into the marketplace for other kinds of opportunities. A good friend of mine was a music minister in several local churches for a number of years. After a season of prayer and seeking God's will, he felt led to relocate his family to a large city where he is being trained to become a public school administrator. Some would say my friend left the ministry. He did not leave the ministry. To the contrary, as a believer, it is impossible for him to leave the large net of ministry since all believers are called to serve within it. He has simply shifted to a marketplace ministry as he continues to surrender to God's leading.

If God is calling you to an equipping ministry, He may

use you in that capacity for life, or He may choose to use you there for a season and then move you into the marketplace to minister. The person who becomes a businessman early in life may finish his life in business. A person's ministry is not measured by what he does, but by what he allows God to do through him, whether he is an equipping minister or a marketplace minister. Paul admonishes the marketplace believers in Colossae to "Conduct yourselves with wisdom toward all outsiders, making the most of the opportunity" (Colossians 4:5). He also exhorts equipping ministers as he writes to Timothy, the young pastor of the church at Ephesus, "Until I come, give attention to the public reading of Scripture, to exhortation and teaching. Do not neglect the spiritual gift within you, which was bestowed upon you through prophetic utterance with the laying on of hands by the presbytery." (I Timothy 4:13-14). All believers must embrace the urgency of God's call and surrender to join Him as He works around each of us through the marketplace as well as within the parameters of the church.

As you contemplate kingdom service, you may be thinking beyond the role of a lay person. Deep in your heart, you may feel a longing to do more than attend others' needs once or twice a week. Are you yearning to dive in head-first and give the majority of your time to ministry? Do you desire for ministry to be your life? If your answer is a burning "yes," then this book is written to help you understand the call of God on your life and move into the next phase of fulfilling God's plan for your life and ministry. You must first realize that ministry comes in all shapes, sizes, and forms. No matter what career or life direction you pursue, you will always have an opportunity to serve and minister to other people. If after reading this material you feel that God may, indeed, be calling you to another vocation besides ministry in a full-time capacity, then do not feel as though you've failed or that God will view you as second-rate. To the contrary, God uses people in all areas of life to fulfill His "big picture" of kingdom work. If you sense that God is not calling you into vocational ministry, you are certainly called into personal ministry through the various avenues in which God has placed you. Rest assured that He has a marvelous plan for your life, and He calls you to humbly serve Him now where He is working around you.

The call to ministry is different for us all, yet the same in so many ways. It is a mysterious, yet clearly undeniable pull in the very core of your being that is impossible to escape. When God invites you to join Him in a special ministry, there is a sense of restlessness that others around you don't seem to experience. It's as though you're at a career day in high school or college faced with a hundred options, many of which are appealing in one way or another. You may be intelligent or talented enough to pursue several of the fields presented, but God is drawing you to something else, something more. You could find some measure of fulfillment in being trained as a teacher, carpenter, engineer, or medical specialist, but none of these areas really delights your heart. Possibly one of these careers interests you, but you have an overwhelming passion to use it in some capacity as a missionary.

Does your family wish to see you pursue a certain career that has nothing to do with ministry? Do your friends express their confidence in what you should do with your life, what you should choose as a career? It's difficult to inform family and friends of your decision when it stands in stark contrast to what you are "expected" to do. You may be afraid that they will think you're crazy, insincere, or even arrogant when you explain that God is calling you to ministry. Possibly you're already in such a position with the people you love if you've made them aware of your plans. Or maybe you are still trying to make sense of it all and cannot bring yourself to utter the words aloud that you know God has a special life assignment for you. Take comfort in knowing that you are not alone in your feelings. I write so freely about them because I felt the same way when I experienced the call of God on my life. In the middle of the turmoil, there is a place of divine peace. It's alright — you can relax! If God is drawing or leading you to some special field of vocational ministry, He will give you an undeniable desire to go and will then provide a way to fulfill the desire He's given you.

Now, please understand that I do not want to beg, plead, or even recruit people for vocational ministry. The ministerial profession is awash with people who have no business being there because they are not God-called, but rather felt the need to help God out in some way. This could not be further from God's design for ministry. To explain it better, I want you to think of your favorite superhero. Is it Superman? Batman? Let's not forget Spiderman. Before you think I've gone off the deep end, stay with me in this illustration. In many episodes that feature famous superhuman crime fighters, the people whom they crusade for beg them to come and save the day. With this stuck in our psyche from childhood, it's easy to adopt that same mindset in ministry – the mindset that says we can save the day in our own strength, basking in our own glory. But God's economy is much different from man's. God fought crime by allowing His only Son to be crucified on the cross of Calvary. Now that the job is done, He invites ordinary men and women to share in ministry to accomplish His kingdom work. You'll never find Superman inviting the average citizen to help him stave off a destructive asteroid in order to save the world! The superheroes in comic books and cartoons may operate alone, but there are no autonomous super ministers in God's plan to save the world. God gently invites, He will never beg or plead with anyone to join the ministry. Yes, we live in a volatile, sinful world. Yes, there are still hundreds of millions of people who have never heard the gospel. Yes, there is still much work to be done! But it is never God's character to beg or manipulate His children into service. We certainly need God, but He does not need us to accomplish His purposes on earth. Rather, He gives us the privilege of partnering with Him in His work! He could share the gospel with one breath, but He allows us to be His spokesmen and women, His witnesses, and even His ministers to a hurting world. So He will draw us, woo us, lead us, and even equip us, but He will never beg.

Unlike the superhero scenario, God prefers to use ordinary men to accomplish extraordinary tasks in demonstration of His power and His glory. In the book of Exodus, God chose Moses, an exiled prince-turned-shepherd, to execute the largest relocation effort in history. Because Moses trusted God, he was given the opportunity to lead over a million people out of bondage toward the freedom of God's promise for those who would obey. In I Kings 18:20-40, the prophet Elijah was engaged in a contest with nine hundred bad-boy priests of Baal. After the pagan priests begged and screamed day and night, their 'god' remained silent, which is pretty much all that can be expected of a block of carved wood. These misguided priests even cut themselves, drawing blood in an effort to get the attention of their god. But one man of God, Elijah, prayed a simple prayer of faith to the one true living God, and God answered spectacularly by raining down fire from heaven. Through God, Elijah not only shamed those who worshipped a nonexistent god, but he brought glory to the one and only true God. After God's spectacular show of power, the people who witnessed it fell on their faces saying, "The Lord, He is God; the Lord, He is God" (18:39). Through Elijah's submission, the glory of God brought people to a realization of truth, and the prophets of Baal were brought to shame. Moses and Elijah are just two of many who proved that God plus one faithful servant is always a majority. Regardless of what the world says, that equation will always work.

Let's visit one more example of God's power and purpose. In Judges chapter seven, Gideon was to go into battle against the Midianites with 32,000 men. That sounds like a fair-sized army, but it was still far short of the mass of Midianites that were gathered against them. Gideon was doubtless concerned and brought his petition to God. After their conversation, God culled out a few hundred soldiers. In fact, Gideon's army was reduced from 32,000 to just 300. Sounds crazy, doesn't it? Yet, when the dust from battle was settled, Gideon declared victory that day, and God was glorified! God's plan often works with odds outside the realm of human possibility, then His surrendered servants are allowed to watch His power and purpose unfold, fully knowing that only God could accomplish such feats. After the battle, Gideon expressed this to the men of Ephraim, "God has given the leaders of Midian, Oreb, and Zeeb into your hands;" (Judges 8:3a). Gideon understood that God uses the few, the ordinary, the surrendered to work against amazing obstacles. This is what God wants to accomplish through all of His servants!

This principle of God using ordinary men to do His supernatural work is illustrated in the New Testament through Jesus' own ministry. He ministered to thousands of people, but poured Himself spiritually into a few ordinary men called disciples. These men unleashed the power and presence of God so that every Jew in their influence and many beyond heard the gospel of Jesus Christ. Likewise, the Apostle Paul was only one man, but he was passionately Christ-influenced and became a strong catalyst for infusing the Gentile world with the gospel, bringing about major spiritual change to those he introduced to Christ. God works with impossible odds so that we'll be fully aware that He alone brings about lasting spiritual impact. The people of

God may always seem to be out-numbered, but God consistently brings glory to Himself through committed servants, no matter the number. Surrender is all He asks, and what He constantly seeks to find in the heart of His children. God is not a bully, a manipulator, or a draft sergeant. You'll not find Him begging or bartering to get a job done. Consequently, He is not threatened by having only a handful of vocational ministers compared to the large needs of the world. If you're feeling pressured to become involved in a lifetime of vocational service because there seems to be no one else to do it, then God is not leading you.

So, how does God lead people into vocational ministry? A look into Paul's life will give us some clarity on the subject. Paul was a highly influential minister and missionary greatly used by the Lord Jesus. In his first letter to the church at Corinth, Paul's greeting states how and why he came to know God's direction for his life. He describes himself in this way: "Paul, called as an apostle of Jesus Christ through the will of God . . . ," (1:1). This simple phrase answers two vital questions about ministry. First, how was he called? Paul says he was "called as an apostle of Jesus Christ." The word *called* means '*to be appointed, to be chosen, to be invited.*' There is no election in heaven or on earth. God chooses those whom He wants to serve in the gospel ministry. If God is truly leading you into vocational ministry, you did not talk Him into it, nor did you invent the idea yourself. In Acts 20:24, Paul tells the church elders on the island of Miletus exactly how he obtained his ministry: ". . . the ministry which I received from the Lord Jesus, to testify solemnly of the gospel of the grace of God." Not only are we chosen to be a minister, but we receive our ministry from the Lord Himself. What a relaxing thought! You don't have to think something up or concoct some sort of ministry. God already has your assignment prepared, and He simply calls you to it. Ministry is about surrendering, not striving.

After confirming how he was called, Paul addresses *why* he was called into ministry. In I Corinthians 1:1, Paul writes that he was called "by the will of God." God is not partial, nor does He love Paul more than He loves other believers. Paul was no more capable or talented than other Christians. In fact, several times Paul mentions in his letters that he was not nearly as gifted a public speaker as were some of his peers. The bottom line is that God's will for Paul was to be an apostle. When God speaks to the heart and draws a person into the gospel ministry, it is His will to do so. He has determined the direction of His kingdom, and He invites us to join Him based on His will. What a privilege! The infinitely all-powerful, all-knowing God has chosen you and me to accomplish His will. *With this knowledge of Who assigns and appoints to ministry, we who hear the call to ministry should examine our hearts and minds carefully to be confident that it is indeed God's call.* Ministry is not a game or a hobby to be tinkered with because you feel somewhat talented or suited for it. To the contrary, it is a high calling centered in the divine and holy will of God. For this reason, I suggest that if you are equally leaning toward other career venues that will fulfill you, explore them, and if you are happily content, stay there.

Christians who are called to ministry through the will of God are not happy doing anything else. Tremendous joy awaits you at the center of God's will. I am convinced that vocational ministry is a privilege handed to you from a loving God. You may be in the critical phase of discerning the call of God on your life. This is a crucial time for you to seek God in a quiet place, to wait on Him, to present yourself available and open to hear what He wants to say to you. I suggest you find a way to remove yourself from the pressures of others so you can pray in honesty and clarity. Then you can begin to hear from God and know with great peace and assurance what is His will.

Discern *Your* Call

Take a few moments to reflect on the main points of Chapter One.

- All Christians have a personal ministry.
- Ministry means "to serve, to attend a need."
- God has placed a deep restlessness in your heart that He has something vocationally special for you.
- God does not need you to accomplish His purposes.
- God will use you mightily when you are outnumbered and overwhelmed by the needs of this world.
- God appoints you for vocational ministry; you don't give Him the idea.
- God assigns the ministry to you; you don't decide what you are going to do for Him.
- If you can do anything besides vocational ministry and live a joyful, fulfilled life, you should do it.

Now respond to these questions with an open and honest heart:

1. Describe your call to ministry. How has God spoken to you concerning His will for full-time ministry?

2. List other careers you are currently involved in or would be happy pursuing. How do these figure in to your perceived call to ministry?

3. How much time in prayer have you spent concerning God's call to ministry for your life? Are you willing to spend more time in prayer? List the specific questions you have concerning the call, and pray over each one, listening carefully for God's direction.

CHAPTER TWO

Fleeting Fad or
Permanent Passion?

*A*s I try to lay out in my mind the events that led to a call to spiritual vocation in my life, I recognize a pattern. The key events in this formation, the ones that really stand out, are those events in which my heart was stirred. They are moments that I was truly excited and moved and touched. Looking back, these events seem to line up, forming an arrow, which has pointed me down the path I am now traveling.

I became a Christian when I was six years old. I remember asking my Dad about Jesus while he tucked my sister and me into bed one night. He pulled out the family Bible – one of those BIG ones that looks really old and has ornate pictures of Jesus and the disciples in it. Using those pictures, dad explained the miracle of salvation to my six-year-old heart. The next day, as I was riding bikes with my best friend, I began telling her about what had happened the night before. I remember being really excited to share with her about Jesus.

Years later, as I grew older, I was very involved in church activities. Many of those activities needed student leaders; students who were willing to speak in public, take charge of a group, and make decisions. I enjoyed doing those things very much. In fact, they seemed to energize me. I soon found myself in a number of leadership roles and realized I was having fun.

One Sunday night I was sitting in a business meeting at church. I wasn't really paying attention to the meeting, just checking my watch and daydreaming a bit. In what can only be described as a light going off in my heart, I realized that I would be fulfilled being in a ministry vocation. I was most energized and satisfied when I was speaking in youth group or serving on a ministry team. Because this happened during a business meeting, I knew I wasn't responding on an emotional high. I truly enjoyed ministry, and it was something I wanted to do with my life and my career.

In college, however, I tried to run from it. I was learning that true ministry is more than giving a moving talk or leading Vacation Bible School. I didn't think I had the extra component that was necessary to be called by God into full-time Christian vocation. I decided to find a "practical" career instead, but the "practical" careers brought no peace to my heart. I finally shared my dilemma with a professor who told me something that touched me at the heart. He told me one way to recognize God's calling in my life was to recognize those things that bring me the deepest joy and that also fulfill the biggest needs in God's kingdom.

The next couple of years were a search into what brought me the deepest joy. Through a series of events, too numerous to explain here, but all of which stirred my heart, I realized that my deepest joy came when I saw people's hearts healed. I was overjoyed and overwhelmed to be part of a moment when a person's heart was healed from the sickness of sin. I was also overjoyed to see fellow Christians live honest, whole lives through the healing power of God and His Word. I wanted God to use me to help heal hearts and build His kingdom.

It may sound simple to say that I feel called into spiritual vocation because the events of my life stirred my heart and led me here. But, I think it is simple. As a Christian, I have a new heart where Christ dwells. I believe I can trust the desires and stirrings of my heart when they match up with the Word of God as Christ's calling in my life. I am excited as He continues to stir and lead.

—Nicole

One phase of discerning God's call to ministry involves the sifting of emotions, thoughts, and ideas to determine if this call is truly God-ordained or just a passing fancy to fulfill a fleshly desire. To illustrate this, I'll share a page from my past. As a teenager, I experienced some turbulent years. I had given my life to Christ at the age of nine, but due to a lack of personal confidence and strained family relationships, I did not live for Christ through my junior high and high school years. I believe it is the result of my mother's constant prayers and the sweet grace of God that I am in ministry today. During my freshman year of college, I began to be discipled by a strong Christian man who showed me how to spend time alone with God, to study the Bible, and to allow Christ to work in my life to use me. I remember coming to the end of myself and asking God to forgive me for living in the flesh. I asked Him to lead me and use me as I surrendered my life and heart to Him. God lifted the spiritual fog that surrounded me. As a result of this spiritual encounter, I began to see and love people as I never had before. When I was fleshly and lacked personal confidence, I became self-absorbed, filled with what the Apostle John calls "the lust of the flesh, the lust of the eyes, and the boastful pride of life" (I John 2:16). When I surrendered my life to the Lordship of Christ, I could see people as Jesus sees them – through eyes of compassion, tenderness, and mercy. This new-found compassion for people would be the beginning of what God would accomplish in my life. When the fog of self and flesh began to lift, God placed a growing restlessness in my heart, drawing me to Himself for a special purpose. The more committed I became in my daily walk with Him, the more I could sense His call to follow Him a step at a time into ministry.

God's call to me was a permanent call; it was a call to follow for a lifetime. When Jesus walked the earth, His invitation to each disciple to follow Him began with following a new Lord: the Lord Jesus Christ. This is where we all must begin. If you are sensing God's call to join Him in His work, then you must first decide to follow *Him*, forsaking other people, positions, things, and ideas that would hinder your commitment. This is the only way you can effectively serve the Lord as a vocational minister. Scripture portrays God-called men and women who left their professions to follow the Lord in vocational service. Others would serve God while keeping their jobs in order to meet financial needs while being involved in ministry. Still others would serve God for a season of time for a specific God-ordained task, returning to their initial professions when God's purpose had been fulfilled. Whether these servants were part-time, bi-vocational, or full-time vocational ministers, they all had one thing in common: each followed the Lord with whole-hearted commitment to the task God had for them. Christian ministry may be full or part time, but the committed Christian's walk with God is characterized by a lifestyle of consistent devotion to God. All Christians, whether in vocational ministry or not, are called to join God where He is and in what He is doing, which requires a willingness to be intimately involved in a relationship with Him.

Throughout scripture, God painted many pictures of committed servants for us, in all shapes and forms of ministry. Moses is one such man. His career as a shepherd was interrupted when God called him to lead the children of Israel out of bondage. This call began a life of ministry as Moses never returned to tending sheep again, but became God's shepherd for the flock of Israel. The Old Testament gives us pictures of prophets who were farmers when God called them out to proclaim His message. As with Moses, some of these servants never returned to their original professions, but others were chosen just for a specific time and then went back to their jobs when their work for God had been accomplished.

In the New Testament, God lets us see into the lives of the disciples as He placed His call on them. When Jesus said to each of them "follow Me," He was calling fishermen, skilled craftsman, even a tax collector – all were men in professions, making a living for themselves and their families. Once Jesus placed His call on them, they never returned to those professions again. They understood the call was permanent and life-altering. Later, the Apostle Paul, a well-trained Pharisee and highly educated Roman citizen, would receive a personal and irrevocable call to follow Christ. This invitation was extended to a man who would not only take up the call, but seize it fully, becoming the most impassioned ambassador of the gospel, ministering to a large part of the New Testament world during his missionary journeys. At one point Paul made and sold tents to support himself while planting churches; however, his passion was making disciples, not making tents.

What about you? Do you feel a growing restlessness that can't be explained away or soothed by external pursuits? It could be that God is speaking to you about His purpose for your life. Whether you are in school or college, already in a career or even with a family of your own, God could be trying to get your attention by stirring your heart and causing discontent with what you are currently seeking in life.

Maybe you've heard God speak at some point earlier in your life, yet you ignored Him, hoping He would leave you alone. There are many miserable Christians in this world who clearly knew the call of God was extended, yet decided against following Jesus' call to vocational ministry. This is a mistake you want to avoid. To separate feeling and emotion from the clear call of God, you must take time to be quiet before Him, seek His will, pray, and study His Word. Only then can you be assured that what you are experiencing is indeed a call to full-time ministry and not just a fad or passing fancy.

For the Right Reason

In the previous chapter, I state that if you can do anything else other than vocational ministry and live a joyful, fulfilled life, do it. On the other hand, some of the most dangerous people in Christianity are people who are not called to vocational ministry but enter the ministry for wrong reasons. These are miserable people who usually leave some trail of destruction in their drive to fulfill a misguided belief that they are here to do something *for* God, thinking that His job is to bless their efforts, regardless of what His plan is for them. For that reason, you must carefully consider your motivations for entering vocational ministry. To help you, let's explore some impure motives that often cause people to enter the ministry:

1. **"My friends and family expect me to go into ministry."** You may be the leader of your church group and have a wonderful heart to serve God in that capacity. Because of your gifts and talents in leadership, others may assume that you are naturally fitted for ministry, but you must beware the pitfall of pursuing vocational ministry based on the expectations of

others. You will certainly set yourself up for failure if this is your primary motivation.

2. **"I can't get a job doing anything else."** To some, ministry must look like a life of ease, a way to get paid without working too hard. Others are lazy and think that ministry doesn't really require special training. How hard could it be? Pastors seem to get a decent salary for just a few sermons and some hospital visits per week. Well, friend, let me just say that this is a dangerously wrong perception, and those who go into ministry thinking it's the easy way out will be shell-shocked and quite miserable. Ministry involves earnest preparation and dedication that is not for the undisciplined or lazy!

3. **"I like people."** While it is good to love people, your calling must be a God-impassioned one. If your motivation is only to help others, you will not endure difficult seasons when you become the target of those who are cruel, critical, and spiteful. You must be dedicated to the call of God and have a passionate heart to serve Him. Only then will you weather the storms of attack by those you serve.

4. **"I love the limelight."** Ministry can seem to be a glowing profession given the amount of attention paid to youth ministers and pastors. They stand preaching and teaching before crowds of people who seem rapt with attention. Then after the service, people stand in line to speak to them, seeking advice, prayer, and maybe even a signature. It may seem that these ministers are up on a pedestal, loved by all, yet there are discouraging times in ministry as well as those mountain-top experiences. For instance, when a church family suffers a death, the pastor is expected to know what to say and do. Popularity can wear thin during church meetings when people say discourag-

ing and hateful things, leaving a pastor disheartened. Entering ministry for the lime-light is a purely selfish motive that will starve you of the stamina necessary to run the race for life.

5. **"It looks fun."** Maybe your youth pastor plans camps, retreats, and other events that get incredible results. Your pastor may oversee a church-wide event that draws large crowds resulting in many changed lives and a great spiritual time for the church or ministry. These are tremendous high points of ministry. Just as there is excitement and even fun in Christian ministry, there are also valleys, low points of discouragement and suffering. Ministry can be very lonely as pastors give huge amounts of their time and energy for little or no reward in this life. Meeting the needs of people and helping them deal with sin can be emotionally and physically exhausting for pastors. You must examine yourself to be sure you are truly called of God for ministry so that you can withstand the various areas of difficult service.

6. **"I can tell people what to do."** To have spiritual authority over people might seem attractive, but a ministry received of Christ cannot be centered on control. Jesus said about Himself, "For even the Son of Man did not come to be served, but to serve . . ." (Mark 10:45). Religious leaders of Jesus' day desired control and power, not unlike a major motivation for some of today's spiritual leaders. Jesus made it clear to them through His life and words that ministry is servanthood. That certainly deflates those who seek to minister because of the power they can have over people. The desire to control and be served is an evil motive for ministry and is adverse to God's design.

7. **"My dad was a pastor."** God does not call a man or woman into vocational ministry based on family heritage, but because He has a unique assignment for the one called. If your parents or an admired family member are vocational ministers, you are not automatically chosen to serve in that capacity as well. There is no ministry gene that is passed down, but well-meaning loved ones can pressure you to follow in the footsteps of a minister in the family. Be careful not to succumb to this pressure. Conversely, don't neglect God's call if you do not have a Christian heritage, thinking that God could never call someone from a family of unbelievers. God calls you because He desires to work through *you*, not on the basis of your family's beliefs or lack of them.

8. **"God will love me more."** Some people think that God loves vocational ministers more than He loves Christians in other professions. Of course, this is unfounded, and a study of scripture will reveal that God's economy of love is boundless and measured equally to all. Following His call into service doesn't mean you are any more or less loved of God. You may have experienced past sin or moral failure and feel that going into the ministry will cause you to be closer to God or more forgiven. Really what you're looking for is an eased conscience. What you need to understand is the unconditional love of God. Forgiveness and grace come freely through Christ, not in a certain career. Your decision to become a vocational minister should not depend on wanting more of God's love or forgiveness. God loves deeply and completely. Trust His love and follow His lead. He will give you assurance concerning the career or ministry path you are to take.

How Do I Know It's A Fad?

When I was a child, fads would come and go. Certain toys, shoes, clothes, or other items would rise in popularity. Stores could not keep enough in stock because of high demand. Then, as quickly as the popularity wave came, it would begin to subside. After a while, the interest would be lost and the fad was over. Several years ago, my oldest son loved yo-yos. Every kid had a yo-yo. Pretty soon there were several different kinds of yo-yos on the market along with instructional videos for how to perform amazing yo-yo tricks. At the height of the yo-yo fad, there were even various kinds of string to buy to improve your yo-yo's performance. It seemed that every room in our house had a different colored yo-yo. Then several months later, I noticed that my son did not pick up any of his yo-yos. His friends did not come over with their yo-yos. No one was interested in yo-yos anymore. As quickly as the wind of yo-yo enthusiasm blew in, it blew out and the interest was lost, leaving piles of unwanted yo-yos lying in retail clearance bins all over town. This is just one example of how a fad starts, builds momentum, peaks for a time, then the focus is lost and the interest level slowly diminishes until the fad dies.

In much the same way, you can be susceptible to faddish feelings and pursuits in your own life. What you feel so strongly about today can fade and fold in the face of slight resistance, leaving you stunned and troubled about your ability to focus on a goal. A litmus test for fads can be applied to strong feelings that threaten to sway you. Take a look at what Paul said to Timothy in I Timothy 1:12, "I thank Christ Jesus our Lord, who has strengthened me, because He considered me faithful, putting me into service." To be faithful means to be consistent, dependable. Faithfulness lasts long after a fad ceases. As a youth minister, I was witness to both fads and faithfulness in young people. In the middle of a week of a youth camp I once led, a student from my youth group said to me, "This is a great week! I love what you do; I think I'll go into youth ministry." After counseling with that bubbling teenager, I realized he was so emotionally charged that he thought he felt a "call" to ministry. My counsel to him was to take some time, pray about it, study the Word, and come back to me in a few months. He agreed. After a few weeks had passed, I asked him how his praying about the ministry was going. He admitted that he had not thought about it since his arrival home from camp. His emotional feeling of having been "called" was just that - a feeling with no basis in God's reality. A true calling spurs a Christian to a higher level of commitment and faithfulness to the call. A temporary feeling that proves to be a fad will fade quickly and will usually buckle under everyday pressures that keep us from following God. Apply this test to yourself: does the call to service exhibit true faithfulness in your life, or is this a perceived call that ebbs and flows with your emotions? Now is the time to seek God in prayer to find His will and forgo your own will.

Are you assured of God's call in your life? Do you know that it is a lifetime call and not a fad? If so, you are ready to take some steps in determining God's will concerning your vocational ministry.

1. **Pray about it consistently**, asking for God's help and guidance.
2. **Stay in the Word.** God will speak to you through the Bible concerning important life matters.
3. **Do a heart check** regarding your motivation for desiring vocational ministry. Restlessness or unrelenting thoughts about ministry will grow stronger, not weaker. You will think about ministry more often and become consumed with wanting to serve God wherever He wants to place you.
4. **Talk with your family about your decision.** If you

are married, discuss it with your spouse. Give your family time to process this information and adjust to your life call.

5. **Talk with a godly friend or minister**, seeking advice about your journey in following God to this point.

6. **At the leading of the Holy Spirit, announce your call to your local church body** under the direction of your pastor. Making your decision public will give credibility to your actions as well as alert a network of believers to hold you accountable. Make yourself available for future preparation and ministry opportunities within your church and community.

Discern *Your* Call

Take a few moments to reflect on the main points of Chapter Two:

- When we walk under the Lordship of Christ, we begin to see people as Jesus sees them – as people who need compassion and who have potential with the grace of God.
- God first calls a person to Himself before He calls that person to a work.
- If you pursue vocational ministry for the wrong motives, you will be miserable.
- If your desire to pursue vocational ministry is a passing fad, the desire of your heart will change, usually under slight pressure or changing circumstances.
- Seek the Lord through prayer, stay in the Word of God, and seek godly counsel as you work through the process of the call to vocational ministry.
- A fad will dissipate; what is of God will grow stronger and will last.

Now respond to these questions with an open and honest heart:

1. What are your motives for becoming a full-time minister?

2. Do your feelings determine your level of commitment to any given task? Examine your feelings about following the call to ministry, identifying emotions that may derail your success.

3. Describe your relationship with the Lord. Are you enjoying intimate fellowship with Him through study of His Word and through prayer? What can you do to improve this relationship?

Part Two:
Determining the Next Step

❦

CHAPTER THREE

Ministry Begins Today

*P*erfectly content. *Those are the words that I would use to describe my career situation before being called into ministry. I had toiled through four years of course work and an intense year-long internship at the University of Tennessee. The hard work had finally paid off when I was offered and accepted the "perfect" job – teaching fifth grade (my favorite age) at a wonderful public school with an awesome Christian principal, an unbelievably supportive staff, and an adorable class of twenty-one. Perfectly content.*

Enter God. I had always had a heart for ministry. At that time, I was filling that niche in my heart through the classroom. No one has ever doubted that the public schools are mission fields, and I have always felt that serious Christian teachers should be considered missionaries. But God was calling me to something bigger – full-time Christian ministry.

It was a beautiful Sunday morning in November. I will never forget it. The sermon was on the sixth chapter of Isaiah, but I never made it past the eighth verse. "Then I heard the voice of the Lord saying, 'Whom shall I send? And who will go for us?' And I said 'Here am I. Send me!'" I know I turned as white as a ghost. I know because my wife,

Shelley, told me as much. Despite the coolness of that Fall morning, I was sweating like it was the middle of July. I knew without a shadow of a doubt that God had called my number. I must have said "Here am I. Send me!" a thousand times in about fifteen minutes.

I remember specifically (and selfishly) praying, "God, if this is real, let Shelley know it, without me having to tell her." I could only imagine trying to explain that I was going to quit the "perfect job" I had held for only a matter of months. I didn't go forward during the invitation. I simply walked out of the sanctuary to the truck without saying a word to anyone. We were headed to Wal-Mart, and I was gripping the steering wheel like a boa constrictor.

Finally, Shelley had had enough. "Jason, what is wrong with you?" I just looked at her and said, "I think you know." With tears in her eyes, she said, "You have been called to ministry, haven't you?"

The next two months were a whirlwind as we braced for a career change. God directed every step along the way. Not one miniscule detail was left undone – spiritual counsel, mentors, position, salary, time frame, support of friends and family. I know that only God could have orchestrated such a scenario. And only God could have convinced me to step outside of what I had considered to be "perfectly content" into what I would soon realize to be His perfect will. "In his heart a man plans his course, but the Lord determines his steps" (Proverbs 16:9).

—Jason

If you were able to stand at a starting line and look down the path of where your life is going in God's design, you would not see a straight, pleasant, tree-lined trail. Rather, you would see many twists, turns, ditches, and rough patches intermingled with pleasant, inviting stretches.

Storms of differing strength would loom ominously ahead. Yet, those beautifully pleasant stretches infused with sweet breezes of God would keep you focused and ready to begin the adventure one step at a time. My friend, in reality you are at the start of a once-in-a-lifetime journey with God as you contemplate your role in vocational ministry. The road that you've traveled so far has brought you to this point. It is littered with debris from past storms and failures, yet it also holds the beauty of God's promise and the seed of service He's planted in your heart. Looking back on the road you've traveled to this point of decision, you must realize that it's all been part of the preparation process to bring you where God wants you. All of these joys, trials, victories, and disappointments God will use to mold and shape your character. Instead of looking at the starting line and waiting to start, go ahead and take the next step on the road you've already been traveling, being careful to follow the footprints of God.

So you're ready to take the next step if only you knew what it was! Actually, it's not a hard step, and it's certainly not spiritual rocket science. It's a step you are most likely already taking, yet don't realize that it involves what God is doing through you now. Many times people who are ready to commit to vocational ministry think they have to wait until they've gotten the education and done the "grunt" work in church ministry. This is a real trap that can lead to wasted time with wheels spinning in no certain, useful direction. What you perceive as your future ministry is not the important focus now. What is important is where you are serving today, or where you can begin serving today. No matter your age – young, middle-aged, older – God is inviting you to get involved now, regardless of your experience or training. He can use everyone in ministry today.

Ministry is Not a Phase: it's a Pattern!

When I was attending seminary in Ft. Worth, Texas, I had the privilege of hearing a message by Major Ian Thomas. I'll never forget what he said that evening as he explained that we are **not** called to be pastors, music ministers, evangelists, etc. Then Major Thomas read from Romans 8:29, "For whom He foreknew, He also predestined to become conformed to the image of His Son, that He might be the first-born among many brethren." That night, something relaxed in me as Major Thomas told us that our primary calling is not to do some future ministry, but rather to live a life of Christlikeness today. I began to focus less on the things I couldn't control and more on becoming the man Christ wanted me to be. Christians can spend so much time wondering what they're going to do and become tomorrow that they don't fully live their lives today. A Christian's change in perspective can mean the difference between being used now or being left to always wonder and worry about where to serve.

Once our perspectives begin to line up with Christ's initiative for us, we understand that we are first called to be conformed to the image of Christ. The word *conformed* means "to be patterned after." A clear example of this can be seen in the construction business. When a special tool or part is needed, a pattern is designed so that all of the resulting parts will be shaped exactly like the pattern. When I worked for a construction company years ago, my boss brought me to a workshop where he showed me a side panel for a cabinet and the pattern for making the panel. Then he explained how to make the panels exactly like the pattern. After he left, I got busy and made about twenty-five panels. They looked great, and I was about to be proud of my efforts when I noticed that I had managed to pick up the wrong pattern lying among several pieces of wood. Every one of my panels was unusable! To say the least, the boss was not happy. My hard efforts were futile because I had patterned all my panels after the wrong pattern.

The same type of mistake can happen to us when we choose the wrong pattern to emulate in ministry. To be effective, you must be patterned after the right Person. Don't put a pastor or a musician or teacher up on a pedestal to become your pattern. Imitating a certain person or a certain ministry position will ultimately weaken and destroy your own ministry. The only safe, sure, perfect pattern is the Lord Jesus; pattern your life after Him. Study the Word of God to learn the character and convictions of the Lord Jesus, then concentrate on taking them on through the power of His Holy Spirit. As Jesus becomes your focus, you can relax and rest in the knowledge that God will lead you and make your path clear. Do not spend precious time worrying about how, when, and where you will minister. And worse yet, don't invent your own ministry and ask for God's approval! Your main goal today, right where you are, is to learn more of Jesus and be conformed to His image. Your future positions, titles, places of ministry are not important now. Rather, make it a priority to pattern yourself after Jesus. Taking on the character of Christ will add power, grace, joy, and peace to your lifelong ministry and to your life as a believer.

It Starts at Home Right Now

Young Timothy had a zealous passion to do great things for God. He had traveled with the Apostle Paul, the missionary of missionaries. When he was preparing to conquer the big city of Ephesus for Christ, he must have felt like the ten spies in Canaan – a grasshopper among giants! Maybe he thought: "Where do I start; what do I do now? I am so young – will anyone take me seriously?" Sounds familiar,

doesn't it? Paul must have sensed these feelings of inade-
quacy in his son in the faith as he assured him with these
words: "Let no one look down on your youth, but rather in
speech, conduct, love, faith, and purity show yourself an
example of those who believe," (I Timothy 4:12). Even
though Timothy was young and inexperienced in ministry,
Paul encouraged Timothy that God had something for him
to do where he was at that time.

When God speaks about vocational ministry, it may be
months or even years away from fruition, yet there is still
ministry to be done today, right where God is working
around you. I am reminded of a fourth grade girl who
wanted to speak to me one night during a children's event.
We went to my office where she told me of her desire to
follow God's leading into missions. She was eager to take a
short-term international missions trip and to see first-hand
the life of a missionary and to serve people oversees. You
see, her enthusiasm for missions resulted in her being available immediately for an assignment. She may have been too
young at the time to take an international trip, but she could
visit a nursing home, feed the homeless at a shelter, or give
a Bible to an unchurched neighbor. As Jesus told us in Acts
1:8, missions starts at home then progresses to the uttermost
parts of the earth. Your immediate assignment is to find
areas in your church and community where you can serve,
then do as God directs.

The extent of your availability and usefulness for the
future is directly linked to your willingness to serve now.
Don't make big ministry plans for the future if you can't take
the time or don't have the desire to serve where God is opening doors today. Sometimes young people are prone to this
pitfall, passing up the obvious yet small areas where God is
urging them to be involved, waiting for the "big break" that
will lead to ministry fame. This happened to a young man
who was once in my youth group. He felt that God was

calling him into full-time ministry. I encouraged him in this and was elated at his decision. As he eagerly spoke of college and seminary plans, it became apparent to me that he was more interested in a future ministry and not a present one. I asked him to become involved in witness training, youth council, and other leadership areas. He always turned them down. When I asked him to accompany me on various mission trips, he seemed to have many excuses to not participate. From time to time I would ask him if he was still "called to ministry." He would smile and say, "Oh, yes," but his ministry was always going to start "tomorrow." While waiting by the road of the future, many great opportunities to impact others for Christ passed him by.

When God leads you into vocational ministry, you are to begin today by becoming an example. If you are still a student, look for areas where God is inviting you to serve in your youth group and church. Be a servant for your youth minister or your pastor. Volunteer for ministries that no one else wants to do. Take opportunities to speak, lead, share, and serve in whatever capacity is needed. After I received the call of God to ministry in my own life, I spoke at rescue missions, directed a church day camp, and served in many other ways. God used each opportunity to shape and prepare me for kingdom work. Next generation ministers participate today. Paul encouraged Timothy to "Be diligent to present yourself approved to God" and to "fulfill your ministry" (II Timothy 2:15; 4:5). Nowhere does he tell Timothy to wait only for the big opportunities to present themselves. Let God open your eyes to areas of ministry around you, and begin now to fulfill your God-given ministry.

Your Ministry is about Relationships

As you contemplate God's call for vocational ministry, you must understand ministry as centered on relationships.

All of us have various gifts, talents, and temperaments. Some are more people-oriented; others are clearly task-oriented. We have to cease looking at ministry through the lens of our own temperaments or personalities and begin to see it through the eyes of Jesus. He is concerned about people. Whether you are counseling one person or speaking to a group of thousands, whether you are organizing a massive event or clearing a table, ministry is about relationships. Let's start by examining your relationships in the following areas:

1. Your present relationship with God through Christ Jesus
2. Family
3. Friends
4. Peers at school or work
5. Other Christians
6. Unbelievers

Everyday we live in a sphere of relationships wherever we are, in whatever we do. First consider the relationship to the One closest to you. How is your personal relationship with Christ? Do you spend time with Him consistently? Are you filled with the Holy Spirit each day, seeking to glorify God with your life? Do you in fact love the Lord your God with all your heart, soul, and mind (Deuteronomy 6:5; Matthew 22:37) or do you merely go through the motions of worship to fulfill an obligation? Ministry must grow out of a love relationship with Christ. Ignoring this crucial step will adversely affect all other relationships and eventually your ministry.

What about your life at home? If you are a teenager, do you have a good relationship with your parents? Are you a peacemaker with your brothers and sisters? If you're married, are you a godly example to your spouse? Do you emulate the life of Christ for your children to see and follow? If you cannot answer yes to these questions, then your focus should be on surrender to God, letting Him work through you to heal broken relationships so you can begin to minister effectively at home. So many children of ministers walk away from the faith because they never saw Jesus in their parents who were busy doing public ministry, but neglected to minister the love and grace of God to their own families. Starting at home is vital to spiritual success!

Friends are many times as close to us as family members. What kind of relationships do you share with friends? Are you encouraging them in their walk with Christ? God places special people in your life to share your journey. Don't take such opportunities for granted. When you cultivate a loving spiritual bond with others, you are creating eternal relationships that can be a valuable source of support and acceptance. If your friends are hearing and seeing a double standard in your devotion with God, they will be inclined to think that God doesn't expect a serious relationship. Be consistent in your walk and be encouraging in your talk. You never know when your example or words will influence another person to answer God's call.

Think beyond family and friends to other areas of influence. If you attend school, do you minister to people there? Do you take the initiative to meet people's needs and be a witness on your campus? Are you an excellent employee for your company? Are you dependable and faithful to your boss? Do you attend to people's needs on the job? Maybe you don't see your life as a ministry, but if you are around people, there is ministry to be done. Don't fall into the trap of putting off obvious ministry opportunities around you with the intent of reaching people in earnest when you become a "certified" minister or missionary. There are no future ministers. You can serve Christ now and make an impact.

When examining our areas of influence, we must consider relationships within the body of Christ. Do you enjoy harmonious relationships with other believers or are there points of contention between you and those with whom you serve? God is clear about our attitude toward other brothers and sisters in Christ. The book of I John explains that one of the identifying marks of a Christian is his or her love for other believers (2: 9-11). If you have difficulty in loving other Christians, then you must examine your faith. God's will is for unity within the body of Christ; it's His way to use us as conduits of love and support so necessary to the health of the church. Great ministry opportunity awaits you as you seek to love and encourage the body of believers within the realm of your influence. Don't neglect these vital relationships!

Beyond the confines of the church and the brotherhood of believers is an obvious avenue of ministry that lies before us each day. We must be actively building relationships with unbelievers in order to bring them to the saving knowledge of Christ. How are you impacting the unbelievers in your part of the world? I'm not talking about a weekly visitation program. It's easy to participate in that, check it off of a spiritual "to-do" list, and then go about our day with no thought of the lost people we come into contact with in every day routines. To have the mind of Christ is to have His compassion for the lost people who cross your path. Of course, sometimes we hesitate to share Christ with the person who has seen us act rude or angry or impatient. For that reason it is so important to walk in the Spirit everywhere we go – not just at church or Bible study. It's a little easier to act like a Christian when around other believers who expect it, but you must take the same care to watch your words and actions around unbelievers who are watching your every move, especially if they know you are a Christian. Don't be afraid to build relationships with unbelievers that will lead to an opportunity to minister to them. Unbelievers are hungry for what you have, and they are drawn to the light within you, so be ready with answers to their questions, and be willing to take time to share the love of God that's so freely poured out on all of us.

Ministry is rooted in relationships; it's about serving people and investing in their lives, building them up, and helping them reach their potential in Christ. This is the reason God just doesn't take us to heaven as soon as we accept His gift of salvation. He leaves us here that we might invest our lives in other people. Paul lived an unusually hard life as a minister of the gospel. At one time he admitted to the Philippian believers that dying would be gain. That is to say, dying would take him out of the difficulty of this world and into the presence of Christ. But look at what he says in Philippians 1:21, 23-25, "For to me, to live is Christ, and to die is gain . . . But I am hard-pressed from both directions, having the desire to depart and be with Christ, for that is very much better; yet to remain on in the flesh is more necessary for your sake. And convinced of this, I shall remain and continue with you all for your progress and joy in the faith." Paul came to realize that God had left him on earth to invest his life in people. Think of those you can invest in, influence, encourage, and love. These are the people whom God has placed around you. Get involved in their lives and minister to them today!

Determine *Your* Next Step

Take a few moments to reflect on the main points of Chapter Three.

- God can use everyone in ministry right now.
- Your ministry is a pattern, not a phase.
- Develop the character of Jesus.
- There are no future ministers; become involved in ministry now.
- Your ministry is accomplished through relationships.
- Your ministry will consist of eternal investments in the people who presently surround you.

Now respond to these questions with an open and honest heart:

1. What are you doing to actively develop the character of Jesus in your life?

2. Examine your relationships as they relate to ministry. How can you minister to the people God has placed in your life?

3. Where are you currently involved in ministry? What other avenues of ministry are presently open to you?

CHAPTER FOUR

Release the Bird

*"She who reconciles the ill-matched threads
of her life, and weaves them gratefully into a
single cloth – it's she who drives the loud-
mouths from the hall and clears it for a different celebration where the one guest is You."*
                                        —*Rainer Maria Rilke*

I became a disciple of Christ at the age of thirteen and
have felt as though God was calling me, as C.S. Lewis
writes, "higher up and further in" nearly every day of my
life since. A "calling" to the ministry comes in different
ways for different people. For me, it has involved a weaving
together of the sort the poet Rilke spoke of. Not the sort that
is a one-time event, but a continual process.
    The ill-matched threads of my life could not have made
me a less likely candidate for Kingdom service. Abused by
my father from the age of six until I was thirteen, child of a
broken family, rebel, thief, liar. . . The list could continue.
However, in calling me to a life of ministry and service, God
has shown me an amazingly freeing, joyful, humbling, giddy
perspective of who and what He is able to use in His

service. In establishing Himself as One able to take the foolish things of this world and confound the wise, He forever turned man-made qualifications for ministry upside down. I felt as though I was not qualified. I'm not. I felt as though the price was too high. It is. And that's the whole point – my decrease ushering in His increase.

God has used me to disciple students as a collegiate minister and as a seminary administrator in mobilizing students, staff, and faculty to serve in missions overseas. Soon I will pack my bags and move into the next season of life. Throughout this time the lesson God has made a vital part of my life is the importance of leaning into the idea of me that He had when He created, formed, and breathed life into me. It is what Paul writes of in the fifth chapter of Galatians: "That means we will not compare ourselves with each other as if one of us were better and another worse. We have far more interesting things to do with our lives. Each of us is an original" (*The Message*).

God's call to ministry is ongoing as long as I walk this earth. It demands "my life, my soul, my all." And so far, the journey has been well worth the price.

—Stacey

As you think about ministry in the realm of relationships, one area must be dealt with before you can move on. It has to do with forgiveness. Leaving issues of forgiveness unresolved will eventually cripple a person's life and ministry. I've seen many people who claim to be brothers and sisters in Christ hold endless grudges that rob them of freedom and joy. If God is leading you into vocational ministry, you must know how to forgive other people and how to accept forgiveness. We are a people who should know how to extend mercy and forgiveness because mercy was extended to us when we did not deserve it. Jesus taught,

"Blessed are the merciful, for they shall receive mercy" (Matthew 5:7). Mercy is simply extending an attitude of grace and forgiveness toward a person who does not deserve it. Since we have been shown mercy by God, now we can demonstrate mercy to other people. In fact, our primary ministry with people is the ministry of reconciliation. Paul writes, "Now all these things are from God, who reconciled us to Himself through Christ, and gave us the ministry of reconciliation" (II Corinthians 5:18). Reconciliation is heavily intertwined with forgiveness and mercy.

First, let's get a clear understanding of the meaning of forgiveness. The word *forgive* comes from the Greek word *aphiemi*. It means "to release" or "to let go." Colossians 3:13 tells us, ". . . and forgiving each other, whoever has a complaint against anyone; just as the Lord forgave you, so also should you." Because we were enemies of God, we needed to be reconciled to Him. Because of our sin, we need forgiveness. Jesus freely forgave us, but how did He do it? Scripture teaches that Jesus reconciled "all things to Himself, having made peace through the blood of His cross; through Him, I say, whether things on earth or things in heaven." (Colossians 1:20). We have peace with God through the blood of Jesus Christ! He died in our place, and through His death God the Father extends loving arms of forgiveness. When we humbly come to Him and admit our need for forgiveness, "He is faithful and righteous to forgive us our sin and to cleanse us from all unrighteousness" (I John 1:9). When you confess sin, you are agreeing with God that you have sinned against Him. After confession, you must accept the forgiveness He offers. Then you can begin a personal relationship with Him through forgiveness. By this we are reconciled to God for eternity.

What happens when we harbor unconfessed sin in our lives and refuse to take the avenues of forgiveness modeled by our Lord? The Psalmist David knew the result and wrote of it in Psalm 32:3, "When I kept silent about my sin, my body wasted away through my groaning all day long." Ignoring sin will not make it go away. Issues of unforgiveness in relationships will grow like a spiritual cancer if not dealt with as sin. Ultimately, these issues will cause the death of effective ministry.

To further understand this, imagine holding a small, sweet songbird with enclosed hands. Immediately you will be aware of its struggle to free itself and fly away. You have two options: open your hands to release the bird or hold on to it, trapping it in the prison of your hands. If released, the bird will fly away and your hands will be free for other opportunities. However, holding on to the bird will eventually snuff out its life and your hands will be unusable. After the bird dies, its stench will follow you wherever you go. People won't be able to see the rotting flesh cradled in your hands, but they will recognize the intolerable smell of death. Because your hands are occupied with this lifeless, odorous bird, you will be forced to pass up opportunities to serve others. In much the same way, we can be guilty of harboring an unforgiving spirit. On the surface, we seem to be vibrant and useable to God, but below that surface a dead, ugly, unforgiving spirit enslaves us, leaving a stench that holds us back from being the ministers God wants us to be. Resolving issues of unforgiveness is a necessary step to take before you can effectively minister.

We can see this illustrated when Jesus issued a call to Peter and his brother Andrew, who would both become part of the twelve disciples. Matthew, another disciple, records this challenge to follow Jesus (Matthew 4:19-20). After receiving the call, these men immediately let go of their nets and followed Him. There were no questions about how to let the nets go, where to lay them down, or what would happen to the nets if they were left behind. The men simply put down what they were holding without hesitation and took up the call to follow. Peter and Andrew understood that their nets would prevent them from fully following after Jesus.

Is there something in your life that you need to let go of so you can follow Jesus with freedom and passion? Are you holding on to the silent rage and bitterness left from a past wrong committed against you? Maybe a person has become so important to you that he or she is keeping you from moving forward. There may be past sins that haunt you, keeping you from spiritual freedom. Are there financial, moral, or ethical situations that you need to reconcile? Open your hands and "release the bird" of sin and past failures. Only then will you know reconciliation and peace in your walk with God, and only then can you be usable to Him. Paul certainly understood the value of releasing the past when he said, ". . . one thing I do: forgetting what lies behind and reaching forward to what lies ahead" (Philippians 3:13). You must follow Paul's example and let go of whatever causes you to look back; then you will be free to take the hand of Jesus and follow Him.

Even though an unforgiving spirit will eventually destroy us, rendering us useless in God's kingdom work, we can be tempted to hang on to it because we're comfortable with it and somehow feel justified in harboring such sin. Our flesh can twist our perceptions so wildly that we even feel God's sanction on our pitiful excuses. We must come clean before God and ask Him to examine us, bringing to light any bits of our sinful past that have not been cleansed. If you are having a hard time releasing bitterness, take a moment to consider the damaging effects of an unforgiving spirit:

1. **A calloused heart**, robbed of compassion and sensitivity for others.
2. **An inward focus** resulting in a lack of foresight and discernment in our approach to people.
3. **A loss of joy** and freedom in ministry.

4. **Physical, emotional, and spiritual problems** leading to exhaustion and even illness.
5. **Anger** toward those you love.
6. **A critical and judgmental attitude** that replaces mercy.

As a young man, I experienced the pain of unmet expectations and learned to release my own bird of unforgiveness. My father and I loved each other while I was growing up, but we struggled to maintain a good relationship as father and son. Both of us kept our feelings toward each other bottled up inside. As a young man in seminary, I lost my mother to cancer. The night my mother passed away, my father and I embraced each other, weeping profusely, and spoke of our love for one another. Both of us commented that we could not remember the last time we had hugged or said "I love you." As time went on, the Holy Spirit of God began to show me issues that I needed to speak to my father about so we could both "release the bird" of past hurt and failures. I visited my father one weekend and explained to him that I had some resentment toward him and needed to reconcile our relationship. Instead of becoming angry with me as I anticipated he would, my father began to cry and told me he was very sorry. My heart was moved as I asked his forgiveness for the times I had been a difficult son. That day the bird of unforgiveness was released for both of us. As a result, I began to relax and accept my father for who he is, and I ceased to struggle with unmet expectations. We began to enjoy each other! Now we express the words "I love you" to each other regularly. Releasing that bird brought great relief and freedom to serve without fearing the hurt of the past.

It's no secret that relationships bring pain. Becoming vulnerable enough to be loved opens us up to all kinds of hurt, resulting in emotional baggage. I think you'd agree that the beauty of relationships is worth the pain necessary to mature them. When you fail to reconcile relationships, you risk losing the very connections that have shaped your identity. You will always carry with you the cumbersome, weighty baggage of pain and fear until you decide to reconcile those issues through forgiveness and love. Only then can you be free to minister as God desires.

Determine *Your* Next Step

Take a few moments to reflect on the main points of Chapter Four.

- An unforgiving spirit will cripple your ministry.
- Forgiveness means "to release or to let go."
- All Christians are called to the ministry of reconciliation.
- An unforgiving spirit causes adverse spiritual, emotional, and physical consequences over time.
- After you've read the illustration of releasing the bird, has the Holy Spirit brought to mind such an experience in your life? What do you need to do to resolve it?

Now respond to these questions with an open and honest heart:

1. Are there any areas of unforgiveness in your relationships? What steps can you take today to reconcile those?

2. Aside from unforgiveness, are there any other hindrances that would keep you from serving God effectively? How can you eliminate them?

3. Do you need to "release the bird" in your life? What are you holding on to that is preventing you from fully following Christ?

CHAPTER FIVE

One Door at a Time

*B*eing the child of a pastor has its perks – one being that no one would ever think me crazy enough to go into ministry having just barely survived growing up in it! But I have. It has been a journey of unexpected turns and unusual adventures. As a young teenager I sensed that God was calling me into ministry, and I was quite sure I would be a medical missionary to China. I told my home church of my plans. I even went through high school on a fast track math and science curriculum. The only problem was that I had absolutely no aptitude for science and math. Music was my thing.

I loved to sing, and the bigger the audience the more I liked it. I went away to college on a voice scholarship and had every intention of going into some kind of vocal performance. I still knew that the Lord had called me into ministry, and I still thought it would be missions of some sort, but He would just have to put the pieces together because I couldn't figure out how it would all fit.

During my junior year the direction of my life changed again. I still loved music but knew I could not make a career of it. I decided to change my major but had no idea which major to choose. I stood at the registrar's office filling out *the paper work for my course of studies. It was a moment that still remains a mystery in some ways. God clearly spoke to me in that moment, and I just scratched my head and said, "Are You sure?" Elementary Education was my new major. I arrogantly informed the Lord that I would change majors, but I would never teach!*

After college, I landed a job teaching! It was short-lived but valuable in my journey towards the future. I ended my teaching career temporarily to join a Christian performing group. I sang on stage everyday – five times a day for six months. It was heaven, yet something still nagged away at me about ministry and missions and teaching.

I consulted my denominational mission board, and they suggested I attend seminary. It was no coincidence that several of my friends from that performing group were headed to seminary as well. It was just the encouragement I needed. I packed up my '77 Toyota and moved to Ft. Worth, Texas, to attend seminary. Once there I declared my interest to be missions and set out on that course of study, thinking again that I might be headed for China after all.

I never went to China. I instead met and married a man that had absolutely no call to overseas missions. Trust me, we struggled with that one! There were two things I know for certain: one, God had called me to do something, and two, this was definitely the man I was supposed to marry. How my call and my marriage would tie together and work out in the future would be up to the Lord because once again I did not see how it all fit together.

For almost two decades now I have been a minister's wife. I have used my professional degree to teach public school on occasion. I have utilized my musical skills in every church we have served. My love for missions has been fulfilled in a number of ways through the local church. I never dreamed that my call to ministry would be fulfilled in part by being married to a minister.

In recent years God has surprised me once again. He has opened the door to speak to women across the country about the truth of God's Word and the joy of the Christian life. All those education classes had been the soil in which God planted a love for teaching the Word of God. Today as I speak to women, I use my music, my education, my love for missions, and my experience as a pastor's wife. All these ingredients add up to the call to ministry I heard so many years ago. God has orchestrated every talent, every class, every ambition, every circumstance, and every relationship to get me to this place for this time and this day. I look forward to the days ahead as the "call" continues to unfold.

— Jennifer

When you've validated your call through careful study and consideration, and you've dealt with issues that would hinder ministry, you may be wondering "What now?" There comes a time when you must begin making some adjustments once you know that God is calling you to vocational ministry. Maybe you've caught yourself staring out the window at school thinking, "I want to be out there where the action is, changing the world for Christ." You might feel less excited about your present employment because God has called you to something else, something more. I assure you these are normal thoughts for those who desire to be in vocational ministry. Most likely, you will soon begin to face transitional periods in your life as you fall in line with what God is calling you to do. These transitions can be frustrating and even frightening at times, but you can meet them prepared and weather them successfully.

God Gives Us What We Can Do Now

Life can be seen as a series of rooms, opening one door

at a time. As you submit to do what you know to do today, God will lead you to the next room in His time. There were times that the children of Israel moved quickly toward the Promised Land. At other times they stayed in the same place for years until the Lord told them to move again. You can imagine how frustrating this could be! Maybe you can relate a bit to the Israelites as you long to be out of school or in a different job, moving forward to help accomplish God's kingdom work on earth. Remember that God's timetable doesn't match yours. What you may interpret as a holding pattern in your life plan may well be an integral part of God's flight plan for you. Don't ask to rush the process, but pray earnestly for guidance and understanding of God's will before making a transition that is not part of God's plan.

In the time since God called me to vocational ministry, He has placed me in a wide variety of leadership roles overseeing the gamut of age groups. I directed a summer day camp for elementary children. Later I served as a youth minister when I was actually not much older than the kids I led. I have served as minister of music, associate pastor, and senior pastor in different churches. God used all of these experiences to make me what He needs me to be in my present ministry role. While these have helped prepare me for my current ministry, they were vital areas of service at the time I was involved in them. I sometimes hear people refer to certain ministry positions as a stepping stone, a promotion or graduation of some sort that will hopefully lead to a more significant role. However, God doesn't see it that way. He gives us the sheep we are designed to shepherd at the right time in our lives. My going from children's ministry to being a senior pastor was not a series of stepping stones. One flock of sheep was not more important than another; all sheep are precious in the sight of God. The years I spent shepherding people of all ages was a great maturing process for me both spiritually and socially, but for me to look at any ministry position as "lesser" or as one more title for my resume on the way to greater success would diminish not only the people I served but the plan of God for those precious people. Ministers and those preparing for ministry must readjust their mindset and focus on the importance of the place God has put them, not on the heights they dream of for their future. The people God gives you to shepherd today are important, whether you shepherd five or fifty thousand. God may use you primarily with children or teenagers. He may give you a classroom or a pulpit in front of an entire church. He may place you on the mission field or give you a traveling ministry of music or speaking. He may give you a ministry of administration or writing or counseling. Remember, God will entrust you with the flock you can handle at the time.

You will take many more "baby steps" than giant leaps as you follow Christ in ministry. As a child, I developed a love for the game of baseball. I have fond memories going to the backyard to play catch with my father. In my immaturity, I would move as far away as possible from my dad so that I could show him how far I could throw the ball. My hopes of impressing my father were dashed most of the time because, in my effort to throw the ball with great speed and distance, it would usually land over the fence in a neighbor's yard. As I retrieved the ball, I realized I was a humiliated child and not a major league athlete. My dad, in his wisdom, would instruct me to stand ten to fifteen feet away from him. As we would throw the ball to one another, it was apparent that my dad was interested in consistency. He would have me throw to his glove. If I threw with good accuracy without his having to move the glove, he would reward me by letting me back up a little farther. There were times that I became impatient, even angry, because I was ready to back up before my father was ready to allow it. My dad knew me better than I knew myself. I had to trust his leadership in my life. Over time, as I became more consistent in the shorter distances, Dad gave me more responsibility with more field to cover. He trusted me with the distance I was able to handle at the time. My father was not concerned with how far I could throw the ball. He was concerned with discipline, accuracy, and consistency.

Our heavenly Father is concerned with our faithfulness in the smaller things as we develop His character and His concerns. Jesus gave the disciples menial tasks during His public ministry. He once told them to bring a sack lunch to Him. Another time he gave them detailed instructions to bring a young donkey to Him. Each small task was followed by a huge demonstration of ministry by our Lord. The small lunch allowed Jesus to demonstrate His glory by His feeding thousands of people with two pieces of fish and five loaves of bread. The colt that was brought to the Master would carry Him into the city for His triumphal entry as He approached Jerusalem for the last time before His death. The ride on the colt would lead to the death on the cross. This death would bring salvation to every person who would turn from sin and self to Jesus.

Concentrate on Your Walk

In May of 1992 when I began my ministry as a senior pastor, I received a call from a dear friend who challenged me with this question: "How do you eat an elephant?" My first thought was, "Who cares" and my second thought was, "With a huge fork." I responded with "I don't know," and what he said next, with that deep Louisiana drawl, has always stuck with me. "Son," he said, "you eat it one bite at a time." What a blessed encouragement he was to me that day. He wasn't explaining the culinary tactics needed to actually consume an elephant. Far from that, he was illustrating a great truth that God never means for us to accomplish everything at once.

Instead, we are to take one step at a time, bathing each one in prayer. Your walk with Christ will determine if you become a strong finisher or a sour failure in Christian ministry. Whether you are still struggling with your call to ministry or you are in the adjustment phase of fresh surrender, your walk with God is essential in your knowing when and how to walk through each door in your life.

James 1:5 tells us "But if any of you lacks wisdom, let him ask of God, who gives to all men generously and without reproach, and it will be given unto him." Through prayer, you can ask God for spiritual discernment regarding difficult situations and decision making. The Bible promises that God will give you wisdom. There are several ways for you to concentrate on your walk at this adjustment stage in your life.

1. **Spend personal time with Christ.** Psalm 46:10 says "Cease striving and know that I am God." Spend time each day praying, being still, listening, meditating on the Word, lifting up your personal concerns. Be consistent, but not legalistic. Focus on your relationship with Jesus. Jesus said in John 10:27, "My sheep hear my voice." At this early stage in your call to ministry, learn to hear the voice of the Master. Learn to love Him.

2. **Be filled with the Spirit.** Ephesians 5:18 warns us not to be under the influence of anything other than the Holy Spirit of God. Seminary professor Dr. Roy Fish likens being filled with the Spirit to exhaling and inhaling. Exhale all the impurities of life through confession. Inhale the influences of the Spirit by allowing God's Spirit to direct and control you each day. Inhale and exhale – it's that simple.

3. **Adopt a spirit of prayer.** All day long you will be confronted with situations, struggles, schedule changes, and decisions to make. Learn to incorporate the principle that Paul writes to the Thessalonians, "pray without ceasing" (I Thessalonians 5:17). An attitude of prayer is an attitude of submission to Christ and is a necessary step to being filled with the Holy Spirit daily. A seminary professor whom I admire once said, "There is no worse stench than that of the flesh trying to be holy." Keeping short accounts of sin and depending on God instead of flesh is a key result of a consistent and genuine prayer life. Don't live your life in the strength of the flesh; you will be exhausted. Rather, inhale the power of the Spirit and unleash it through committed prayer.

4. **Search out godly friends.** You will become like those whom you choose as friends and confidants. Paul warns us in I Corinthians 15:33, "Do not be deceived: 'Bad company corrupts good morals.'" Psalm 1 begins, "How blessed is the man who does not walk in the counsel of the wicked." Godly people are inclined to give godly counsel and keep you accountable to truth. Worldly people give worldly advice. They will encourage you to run when God expects you to stand strong; they will counsel you to stay in the presence of sin when God expects you to flee. Godly friends help lead you in the way of righteousness and support you in ministry. God will bring the right kind of friends to you – just follow His lead.

If you want to finish strong, concentrate on your walk with Jesus Christ. Do not try to see the entire picture of your life. Rather, seek God's face with your whole heart, allowing Him to open the doors you should walk through. Also allow Him to seal the doors you should not walk through. As Paul was on his way to Rome, he was placed under house arrest, chained to a praetorian guard. He confesses in Philippians, "Now I want you to know, brethren, that my circumstances have turned out for the greater progress of the gospel, so that my imprisonment in the cause of Christ has become well known throughout the whole praetorian guard and to everyone else, and that most of the brethren, trusting in the Lord because of my imprisonment, have far more courage to speak the word of God without fear" (1:12-14). Many prison guards came to Christ because God allowed Paul to be imprisoned. If you have a consistent walk with God, you will see a change of plans or difficult circumstances not as hindrances, but rather the hand of God working in your life so that you might influence someone else for the cause of Christ. Become consistent in walking with Jesus and hearing his voice. Your walk of obedience will enhance and empower your service to God.

Determine *Your* Next Step

Take a few moments to reflect on the main points of Chapter Five.

- God will open one door at a time.
- Be faithful in what you know you can do right now.
- No task is insignificant when you are being faithful to God.
- Concentrate on your daily walk with Christ.
- Do not try to see the whole picture of your life, but focus on what God wants to do in you today.
- Circumstances that you perceive as hindrances can be used of God to further His kingdom purposes.

Now respond to these questions with an open and honest heart:

1. List the areas of service you've already been involved in. How can these be used by God to assist you in your current ministry pursuit?

2. Where do you need to concentrate on your walk?

3. Identify circumstances that you have so far seen as hindrances. Could these be part of God's plan to move you further into the ministry He has planned for you? How so?

CHAPTER SIX

Prepare, Prepare, Prepare

*T*here are three aspects of the life of any minister: the beginning, the journey, and ultimately the finish line! Each of these is of the utmost importance. To help me in these aspects, God has given me one constant figure who has been a faithful counselor and mentor for the sole purpose of seeing me minister with excellence until my race is done.

During my sophomore year in high school, my brother Richard and I were invited to attend a small Bible study on a Wednesday night. Little did I know that my life would be changed forever as I heard the message of God's salvation and love. We did our best to settle into bed that night to no avail. God was at work, convicting our hearts to receive Christ and that's exactly what we did. Together, we knelt down beside our beds and prayed to receive Jesus Christ as our Savior and Lord!

The next Sunday morning, we returned to the church we had attended as young children. We walked right up to our new Sunday School teachers and told them that we needed to be baptized immediately. Before long, I was actively involved in our youth ministry, experiencing the greatness of

---

God through intimate times of worship and discipleship.

The student ministry was on fire for the glory of God under the leadership of the man who would become the faithful counselor and mentor in my journey. During the next three years, this man led Richard and I to maturity in Christ as we were taught to study God's Word and to be actively involved in sharing our faith in Christ and ministry. By the end of my junior year in high school, God's Spirit began to impress upon me a specific calling into full-time Christian ministry. After speaking with my mentor and following his counsel, I waited on the Lord to give me a clear and definite promise that this was His will for my life. In just a brief time, God did give me this assurance through many different passages of Scripture and times of prayer.

I am now on my journey of ministry with the momentum of a great beginning! As a church planter, I am seeing God do what only He can do as people are being won to Jesus Christ and lives are being turned back to the heart of God. With the encouragement of strong mentors and the faithfulness of the Lord, I am confident that I will finish the course that God has given me.

No matter who you are, no matter what your age, seek the face of God and wait patiently upon Him to affirm the calling of Christian ministry. Once this calling is assured, do your best to begin well, enjoy the journey, and stay the course to the end!

—Chris

A call to vocational ministry is a high calling. When God sets you apart for a significant purpose, He deserves the very best you can offer with your life. Respected pastor and author John McArthur said "If we will take care of the depth of our ministry, God will take care of the breadth of our ministry." You must make preparation a priority, refusing short cuts that would undermine your effectiveness.

Training with Instruction

Many career tracks require two to ten years of preparation. We all like to be assured of a professional's qualifications to perform a service required. When I go to the dentist, I do not ask to see the dental hygienist's diploma. Because I know the dentist, I trust him to hire certified personnel. Imagine that, while the hygienist is cleaning my teeth, she says, "I have always wanted to be a dental hygienist. I've never been trained to do this, but I've had my own teeth cleaned before and I've watched a few times, so I'll try to do the best I can on your teeth." I guarantee you I'd be out of that dental chair as fast as humanly possible, and no one else would venture to sit there either. Now rest assured that my dental hygienist is, thankfully, very qualified and adept, so I totally trust the quality of her work. Proper training is an essential in the people we visit for various services! What if you had an expensive car needing maintenance? Would you take it to someone who had never been trained and certified to perform the work on your car? What if you needed surgery? Would you go to a compassionate person who had never been to medical school? Of course you wouldn't! All the compassion in the world could not take the place of adequate training when you're about to be cut open. These careers are wonderful and provide the necessary services that keep us healthy and our lives up and running. Professionals take their training seriously and most perform their jobs with excellence; however, these are temporary services. Ministry is set apart in that it is not a temporary service; it involves eternity. Ministry is not concerned with teeth or cars; ministry focuses on souls. How much more serious, then, should a person be in preparing for his or her ministry service!

If you sense that God is leading you to care for souls in vocational ministry, you should be trained to become the most excellent servant of God you can be. I have heard people say to someone newly called to ministry, "Don't go to school, it will just mess you up." Granted, there are some institutions that may do more theological harm than good, but there are many more fine schools and places of training that excel in equipping next generation ministers. Young people who aspire to become doctors are never told to forgo schooling because it may "mess them up." To the contrary, they are urged to get the best medical training available. A person called to ministry should feel the same drive and urgency to prepare for service to souls.

In your haste to get into the ministry, don't quit school or your present job in order to pursue church work. The next step for you is training and preparation. When Jesus began calling the disciples, He told two of them to "Follow me, and I will make you fishers of men" (Matthew 4:19). Notice the response when they heard the call: they immediately put down their nets and followed Him. He did not lead them into a public Christian service position at first; rather, He led them to training, and they followed. He taught them for three years before they obtained any kind of public ministry of their own. So, the surrender to the call of vocational ministry demands the called one to surrender to excellent preparation. Jesus unfolded a three-year plan with the disciples which involved the following steps:

- **Learn the purpose of service from Me.** Jesus spent many hours teaching His disciples about servant-hood as the basis of ministry.
- **Watch Me serve.** After teaching about servanthood, Jesus modeled the role of a servant on numerous occasions as He met the various needs of people around Him.

- **Serve with Me.** An invitation followed the training and modeling of servanthood. Jesus asked the disciples to minister with Him in meeting the people's needs, and He remained available to them for further instruction and evaluation.
- **Serve.** After Jesus' death, resurrection, and ascension, the disciples began their public ministry under the power and influence of the Holy Spirit. At this level, they were trained to continue the work of the kingdom without the physical presence of Jesus. Their ministry preparation while in Jesus' presence had equipped them to spread the gospel into the heart of the Greco-Roman world.

The Apostle Paul obviously understood the importance of preparation for ministry. According to most scholars, Paul was mentored in the faith during a three year stint in the Arabian desert following his dramatic conversion experience. This training better enabled him to become an impassioned pioneer missionary, starting many churches in the Greek world and writing over one-third of the New Testament. Even with these good examples you may still be thinking that Christian training is overrated. It's tempting to just dive in head-first and ask God to give you the words and ideas as you need them. That may sound like a good plan, especially since it avoids years of training. But an important truth about training cannot be overlooked. II Peter 3:15-16 explains, ". . . just as also our beloved brother Paul, according to the wisdom given him, wrote to you, as also in all his letters, speaking in them of these things, in which are some things hard to understand, which the untaught and the unstable distort, as they do also the rest of the Scriptures, to their own destruction." The Bible tells us that a person called to ministry who is not properly trained to handle the Word of God with godly accuracy, nor the souls of people with godly integrity, can actually destroy the ministry instead of prosper it. Do you desire to actually bring more harm than good to the cause of Christ? There is a clear danger of doing just that if you ignore warnings to be properly trained. God's desire for His servant is to know His Word and how to accurately handle it so that there will be no distortion of His miraculous grace and love (II Timothy 2:15). In the near future, you may be dragging yourself to yet one more class wondering if you're wasting time. When those thoughts arise, take a moment to remember Paul's exhortation and the reason God requires training in truth, and be diligent in rising to the challenge of your call.

Paul was an encourager to young, newly-called ministers just like you. This is especially seen in his exhortations to Timothy as he wrote, "All Scripture is inspired by God and profitable for teaching, for reproof, for correction, for training in righteousness; that the man of God may be adequate, equipped for every good work" (II Timothy 3:16-17). It is very important to know what you believe and why you believe it. The major tenets of the faith keep us from wandering from the truth. Be involved in Bible training from good, reputable teachers. Do all you can in the early stages of your ministry to go deeper into the Word of God.

Training Through Imitation

Most children go through a phase of imitation. My youngest son certainly did, and he drove his older brother nearly insane for a while. The younger brother would try to mimic the walk, talk, and even mannerisms of his older brother. In fact, sometimes he would repeat words and try to do everything exactly like his big brother. Some of this was done purely to irritate his brother. However, much of the imitating grew out of admiration and respect. The little one was saying with his words and behavior, "I want to be just like you, brother."

When you were a child, was there someone bigger than life that you wanted to emulate? Paul said of himself, "I exhort you therefore, be imitators of me" (I Corinthians 4:16). At first, this sounds like an arrogant statement. "Look at me, I'm better than Jesus." But Paul was not attempting to take attention away from Jesus. Quite the contrary! He was encouraging these new believers to look at Jesus *in* him so they would have an earthly mentor. If you want to see the character of Jesus here on earth, find a godly man or woman to imitate. John Maxwell, founder of Injoy Ministries, challenges attendees at his leadership conferences to interview ten people in the desired ministry field who have thriving ministries. A young man desiring to be a pastor should interview several godly men who have Christ-like characteristics and who shepherd vibrant, growing churches. Paul tells believers to ". . . join in following my example, and observe those who walk according to the pattern you have in us" (Philippians 3:17). Paul explains that other believers should use the godly attributes in his character and ministry for their own Christian walk and success in leadership. In many areas of life we're told not to copy, and we may even be punished if we do. For instance, recording someone else's song and calling it your own is a violation of copyright laws that will certainly bring a lawsuit. Taking credit for a manuscript written by another person is plagiarism. But these parameters do not apply to imitation in the realm of Christianity. If you incorporate the Christ-like character and abilities of a mature Christian into your own life, it is called discipleship and it reaps not punishment, but eternal reward as you apply them to your ministry.

In a conversation with His disciples, Jesus said, "You call me Teacher and Lord; and you are right, for so I am. If I then, the Lord and the Teacher, washed your feet, you also ought to wash one another's feet. For I gave you an example that you also should do as I did to you" (John 13:13-15). Jesus clearly uses Himself as an example of a true servant-minister. He is still leading by example today *through* ministers who are submissive servants of His kingdom purpose. Find people who exhibit Christ-like character, who serve in a ministry you are presently interested in, and meet with them. Ask them questions about their walk with God, the ministry they serve in, the call of God on their life. While you examine aspects of their ministry and Christian walk, remember that you are not to become a clone of their style and personality. God has given you a distinct personality and has gifted you specifically to accomplish His will through you. He will use you in a special, unique way to impact other people's lives. Also avoid comparing your ministry results to those of a mentor. Finding a mentor is vital to your training, but constantly measuring yourself to someone else's accomplishments will usually serve to discourage your own efforts. For now, concentrate on submitting yourself to a godly mentor so you can learn and incorporate certain aspects of his or her life into your own life and ministry.

As you consider training through a mentor, understand that there are three areas of life engaged in emulation. When these specific areas are developed and matured, ministry can reach its full potential. These areas cover character, competence, and capability.

Character. At the core of your heart is the motivation that drives what you say and do. Jesus said that where a person's treasure is, that is where you will find his heart's devotion (Matthew 6:21). What do you care deeply about? What motivates your behavior? What are your convictions about life, death, mortality, and spiritual values? These elements fuel the fire to make you who you really are. In other words, they form your character. Can you be trusted? Are you honest? Do you treat people equally and with integrity? Paul said in Philippians that we are to show affection, love, selflessness, and humility (Philippians 2:1-4). These are all building blocks of Christ-like character. How does a person incorporate the character of Christ? "Let this mind be in you which was also in Christ Jesus, who, being in the form of God, did not consider it robbery to be equal with God, but made Himself of no reputation, taking the form of a bondservant, and coming in the likeness of men. And being found in appearance as a man, He humbled Himself and became obedient to the point of death, even the death of the cross" (Phil. 2:5-8 NKJ). The character of Christ is demonstrated by extreme servanthood. This extreme attitude of Christ-likeness produces an extreme behavior of Christ-likeness, what we all should aspire to become in character

Competence. Webster's New Collegiate Dictionary gives several definitions of this word. The primary definition is, "A sufficiency of means for the necessities and conveniences of life." The root meaning of the word is "*to be suitable.*" How can you be suitable for ministry? How do you know that you are competent as a Christian minister? Three components put us on the path to competence in ministry and in our Christian walk:

- **Grace provides spiritual competence**. God's grace was given to you at the time of salvation. As He demonstrated unmerited favor to you, you can demonstrate an attitude of grace toward others.
- **Knowledge gives intellectual competence.** As your knowledge increases, your ministry to people is empowered by truth. As your awareness of God's truth is revealed, your ability to meet the needs of people increases.
- **Wisdom undergirds relational competence.** In Proverbs, we learn that "the fear of the Lord is the

beginning of wisdom" (Proverbs 9:10). This book also instructs that wisdom and understanding are necessary tools for a successful life. A wise and discerning heart can offer competence in decision making, problem solving, and caring for others.

Grace, knowledge, and wisdom combine to make a minister competent. God's primary interest isn't in choosing the intellectually elite for His purpose. However, be careful not to use this as an excuse to cover laziness. While God prizes a submissive heart, He expects you to be well-prepared to the full extent of your mental capabilities. II Peter ends by admonishing believers to grow in grace and knowledge. The experiences of life, coupled with knowledge of truth, will produce wisdom and understanding. You must allow God to develop you into a competent Christian leader.

Capability. A capable minister develops his or her talents, temperaments, and giftedness by using them to edify the body of Christ. All of us are given abilities to serve and lead in the way God intends. While we must know and develop our abilities, we must also realize our limitations. During my earlier ministry as a student pastor, a young man named Howard joined our church family. Having come from a broken home, Howard appreciated the attention given to him by Christian men in the body. He was shy when he first became involved with the youth group, but he slowly gained friends as his confidence in relationships with other kids grew.

As Howard's new confidence gained momentum, I was confronted with an interesting situation one Wednesday evening during our mid-week student worship. This service, called LifeSource, drew several hundred middle school and high school students. It consisted of a praise band, testimonies, video clips, drama, and special music. Much of the worship was student led. At one such service, Howard approached me asking, "Can I sing next Wednesday night?" Our worship leader never auditioned anyone who wanted to participate, so I told Howard to be ready to sing. At the next LifeSource service, the room was packed with teenagers singing during the praise and worship time. At the appropriate time, Howard stepped to the microphone, nodded to the soundman, and waited to sing as the accompaniment track began. I'll never forget the tune I heard as Howard began to sing. It's burned in my memory along with the expressions of the teenage audience who had been looking on in support and pleasantly waiting to hear Howard. When he opened his mouth, unusual sounds came forth, the sounds of a young man who was nowhere close to the key of the music. It was monotone at best; actually it was much worse that that.

As Howard did his best to sing, the young people looked first at him, and then at each other, in disbelief. They didn't know whether to laugh or cry. My initial thought was if I had heard something like that out in the woods, I would have shot it to put it out of its misery! Most of the students looked at Howard with respect and patience. The worship leader looked at me as if to say, "I'll unplug everything, you get the lights, and we'll go home." That five-minute song seemed to last for forty-five minutes. Howard squawked the same awful tone during every verse and chorus before the song finally ended. We all then breathed a sigh of relief as the worship band got the service back on track.

I sat near the back of the room in stunned silence for the rest of the service. After the service ended, I felt a tap on my shoulder and there was Howard, smiling and eager to talk to me. I was ready to console him, thinking that he must be chagrined, knowing how badly his song went. He asked the dreaded question, "How did I do?" I was a surrogate father of sorts to Howard. My opinion meant a great deal to him. I had spent months encouraging him, and he was enjoying newfound confidence. I would have rather taken a beating than answer his sincere and childlike question. To make matters worse, it dawned on me that Howard was the only one in the room that night who had not realized that his singing was comparable to the sound that cows make when their young calves are weaned. I had made a commitment never to lie to the students I led, no matter the cost. Now I had to stand up to Howard and say, "We need to talk." He said "Okay," beaming as he went to fellowship with other students.

That night was not an appropriate time to tell Howard that I would have him arrested if he ever got close to that microphone again. He scheduled a time to meet later that week. As the day of his appointment came, all morning I rehearsed what I would say to him. I would speak the truth in love, being tender yet firm; loving, yet forthright. I would let him down gently, discussing with him other areas of service where he could pour his gifts and talents, and all would be well. That seemed like a good plan, but before I could open my mouth to address Howard, he blurted out, "God is calling me into the music ministry!" I needed some Pepto Bismal! This was getting out of hand. As he explained his desire to be a music evangelist, I could only think of the pain he would inflict on other congregations. I couldn't let that happen to other people! I forgot the truth in love speech and said something like, "Howard, you are not called to music ministry; the song was terrible." He looked at me as though I had just said, "I hate you." Now it was his turn to look at me with disbelief. He reprimanded me, telling me that several kids let him know what a blessing his song had been. I told him they were just being nice. Howard had totally trusted me, depending on me for strength, confidence, and encouragement. Now he was crushed, his heart churning with a mix of anger and disappointment as he turned to leave without saying good-bye. I felt terrible.

Proverbs tells us that the wounds of a friend bring

success (27:6). I could have easily appeased Howard that day, patted him on the back, pretended that he would have an effective music ministry. But that would have only proven to set him up as the community laughing-stock. Several days later, Howard came back to thank me for being honest with him. Howard did eventually surrender to vocational ministry. He graduated with a master's degree in theology and has become an articulate preacher of the gospel. He's even spent time in Indonesia sharing the gospel with a people group who had never seen a foreigner, much less heard the name of Jesus the Savior. That bump in the road during his teenage years was just one step in steering him toward the ministry he was truly capable to do.

No amount of enthusiasm can take the place of capability. Knowing strengths and limitations is a vital quality of effective ministers. They understand the importance of capability and celebrate these strengths, using them to edify the saints for the glory of God. On your journey to ministry, ample opportunities will arise for you to test your own capabilities. Heed the advice of godly believers whose straightforward feedback will help to sharpen and polish your skills.

Study the character, competence, and capability of your mentors, learning from their mistakes as well as their successes. Several men and women in our own church family feel led into full-time Christian service and often seek advice from me. One of the things I tell them about learning from me is, "Learn what to do and use it; learn what not to do and avoid it." You can learn from weaknesses just as you can learn from strengths. Not long after the Desert Storm confrontation in the Persian Gulf, General Norman Schwartzkoff was interviewed by a reporter who asked, "What do you believe has made you such a great general?" His answer was simple. He explained that through the years of his military career, he was under some very incompetent and decadent commanding officers. He observed their lack of character and competence, and avoided implementing those elements into his life. From this, we can learn that God orchestrates everything in our lives, even bad examples, to show us how to lead effective and purposeful lives.

Of course, the only perfect mentor is the Lord Jesus. Be careful not to exalt other people. Only Jesus is worthy of exaltation, and we are to follow His supreme example in service and servanthood. The Bible speaks of earthly models we can look to now for instruction and reassurance that we are following the right path in ministry. In II Thessalonians 3:9, Paul understood how important it was for him and his ministry partners "to offer ourselves as a model for you, that you might follow our example." Part of your formation as a next generation minister is to find a ministry model. Be sure to find a mentor who models godly character, capability, and commitment to God's call. A person who models a love relationship with Christ will show you how to serve the Lord with excellence.

Determine *Your* Next Step

Take a few moments to reflect on the main points of Chapter Six.

- Preparation equips us to be used by God as He chooses.
- We are given an eternal responsibility to care for the souls of people, and must obtain the proper instruction and training to help us become effective ministers.
- Jesus called His disciples to a time of instruction and training before they were given a public ministry.
- Good preparation is vital in order to advance the cause of Christ and not hinder it.
- Understanding the tenets of the faith is a vital step in your progress to become a Christian leader.
- Emulate the Christ-like qualities of a godly person.
- You must develop character, competence, and capability in order to reach your full ministry potential.

Now respond to these questions with an open and honest heart:

1. Do you currently have a mentor in ministry? If not, who can you approach to become a mentor?

2. Are you aware of your strengths and weaknesses in ministry? If so, list them. You may want to discuss this with another person who will give you honest answers.

3. What steps will you take to prepare for effective ministry?

CHAPTER SEVEN:

Beware of Cold Water

I was raised in church and made a public profession of faith at the age of eleven. My walk with Christ was what I considered normal, but I did not really consider entering the ministry until nine years later when God really spoke to me. During my late teenage years, I began to focus my attention on things other than God. I began to consider the different paths my life might take as I looked forward to college. I was concerned with two things: my happiness and a solid financial future.

As I went to college, I was happily headed down the path of my own choosing. I went to a True Love Waits retreat with a friend. We were there only because we were visiting some people. I was not involved in the retreat, but as I listened to what the speaker said, God moved in my heart. I knew undoubtedly that God had spoken to me and that He had called me into His service.

After talking with the youth minister at my home church, I was still in the dark. I knew that God had called me, but I did not know what I had been called to. He told me to wait on the Lord. It was what I did not want to do, but I did not really know what else to do, so I did it. I waited. I did not change my major in college. I just waited.

The following summer, I helped out in the activities of our youth group. I led Bible studies and went on trips. We went to a World Changers mission trip to Charleston, South Carolina. I worked with the youth all week. I prayed for the youth all week. Then, at the final commitment service, I was praying for the youth I had come with. During the invitation, something happened to me that I cannot explain. I moved from the back of the chapel to the front, only I do not remember moving. I was in the back praying, and then I was at the altar, weeping. I knew that God again had spoken to me. This time, I had what I had been waiting for. God's desire was for me to work with youth. There was no doubt in my mind. So, that is what I committed my life to.

I was ready to change the world, one youth at a time. But once again, I needed to wait. I tried to get a position in several churches, but I could not. It was nearly nine more months before I was called to a church.

Several years later, I realized that God was leading me away from youth ministry and into another facet of ministry. I do not know what God will allow me to do before I die, but I am convinced He called me to ministry, and I am committed to serving Him wherever He leads.

—Dave

Have you ever heard the statement, "Finish what you started"? Sometimes it's easier to start a project than to finish it. As you read this final chapter, it is important for you to know that saying "yes" to God regarding your commitment to vocational ministry is only a part of the picture. The ministry God has entrusted to you is a life calling. The process can be likened to a batter in a baseball game who hits a home run over the fence. He must run around all the bases and step on home plate before his hit is declared an official home run. So you, too, must do what lies before you to fulfill the awesome responsibility of God's call, regardless of circumstances, opposition, or temptation.

As you covenant with Christ to serve Him in vocational ministry, understand there will be very deep valleys of discouragement in your life. Times of refreshing and life-changing events will also occur, but you must realize that God has called you to a ministry that will not be without spiritual attack. Paul said in Ephesians 6:12, "For our struggle is not against flesh and blood, but against the rulers, against the powers, against the world forces of this darkness, against the spiritual forces of wickedness in the heavenly places." Satan, the evil one, has been granted permission by God to roam the earth seeking whom he may devour (I Peter 5:8). He will use any available person, resource, or weakness to keep you from finishing well. In this pursuit of destruction, many weapons are launched against the person who feels called to vocational service. Let's look at some of them:

Spiritual Attack from those You Love and Respect

The call to God's service can sometimes be met with spiritual attack from the people you least expect would attack you. One instance I can relate happened when I was a student pastor. We took two hundred young people to Florida where we experienced a glorious week of revival and life-changing decisions. The last day of camp, a high school girl expressed to me her exhilaration about what God had done in her life. She professed to me, "God is calling me to vocational ministry!" Her countenance radiated as I affirmed her. Shortly after, we all loaded the buses for the twelve hour trek home all night. Sleep was rare due to singing and chattering on the buses. Early the next morning, we pulled into the church parking lot where dozens of happy parents stood ready to greet their teenagers and retrieve their luggage.

I happened to be on the same bus with the young lady who had shared her heart with me regarding vocational ministry. Even though she was exhausted, she bounced off the bus with exuberance and found her mother. She said with excitement, "Mom, there is something I want to tell you!" At that point, her mother cut her off and snapped, "Get your suitcase and come to the car; your father and I are getting a divorce." I watched with disbelief as the young lady almost fainted at the horrible news. Her mother's words were painfully disabling. I wanted to cry for her as I watched her leave. Her life, her destiny, and her family as she knew it were changed in a sixty-second conversation. The girl's parents did divorce, yet she remained faithful to the youth group. She did not allow the pain and discouragement of her situation to disrupt her commitment to God's call. She later graduated, attended college, and now serves as a pastor's wife with a family of her own. Years later, God honored her prayers by reconciling her mother and father, leading them to remarry. God was not taken by surprise at the turn of events in her life, and He remained faithful to her in the dark days that followed camp that year.

As you commit to serve Christ vocationally, you may receive "cold water" in the form of cold words from someone you love. A trusted friend may try to talk you out of being in vocational ministry. I once knew of a mother and father who threatened their daughter with never speaking to her again if she became a missionary. Sometimes in a twisted way of thinking they are protecting their children, parents try to act a little like God and manipulate their children into following a plan other than God's. But God knows what is best for each of us, even beyond what our parents or significant loved ones know. This missionary-minded girl eventually went to the mission field with her husband in obedience to God's call. Incidentally, her parents accepted this decision, and later traveled a great distance oversees to visit their daughter and her family (ah, the power of grandchildren). For those who face an attack from loved ones, know that if you are truly God-called, He will orchestrate all events, including attacks, to the benefit of your service within His will.

If you're willing to face the challenges of ministry, you must ready yourself for such cold water attacks. Remember that God will always sustain you as you remain faithful. Ministry is a high calling. If God has really given you a ministry, nothing can stop you; no one will be able to talk you out of it. Obey the Lord and let Him take care of your circumstances. In Jesus' day, many families would disown a son or daughter who became a follower of Christ. Whether your family or friends are supportive or not, God will always bring new people into your life to love and encourage you. People often say discouraging words because they are afraid or they don't understand. Most people will come to accept your decision in time. Be faithful and obedient in what God has called you to, allowing Him to use even cold water attacks to strengthen and mold your character.

Spiritual Attack from Personal Hardship

Some believe that once you give your heart to Christ, you won't face any more problems. Surely you have been a Christian long enough to know that becoming a Christian invites even more problems associated with peer pressure, temptation, and relationships. Christians who are called to vocational ministry can be assured that they will suffer hardship and difficult times. You may be discouraged now about something in your life. In II Corinthians 1, Paul was so dismayed about his circumstances that it caused him to sink to a very low point. He describes this in verse eight,

"For we do not want you to be unaware, brethren, of our affliction which came to us in Asia, that we were burdened excessively beyond our strength, so that we despaired even of life;" Paul's emotional agony shows that he was well-acquainted with suffering in ministry.

Think of this: the great missionary Paul despaired of his own life. Does this mean that even so-called "Super Christians" suffer to the point of despairing? Oh, yes. These times of despair deepen and build character. Personal or ministerial circumstances can dishearten, and people can be mean and critical. A family or personal health crisis can bring despair. Important plans can be altered, causing confusion and discouragement. Paul's journey is an example of this, as his plans to share the gospel in Rome were put on hold when he became arrested and imprisoned en route. He *did* get to Rome, but he was stranded in prison, which was not exactly his idea of how to spread the gospel to the Romans. Didn't God want Paul to spread the good news of Christ to the people of Rome? Yes, definitely, but another group of people were also needy and ready to hear the gospel: the praetorian guards.

In Paul's day, there were two ways to be imprisoned. The most dangerous criminals were put in a jail cell. The less dangerous criminals, like Paul, were handcuffed to prison guards. Paul shared Christ with the guard that was shackled to him. I can imagine that every time a guard accepted Christ, a new guard would be assigned to Paul. It wasn't long before many of these guards became believers because they had been chained to Paul. What if Paul had spent the whole time complaining to the guards about not being able to fulfill his mission to the Romans? Doubtless, he would have been ineffective. Instead, he saw his imprisonment as an opportunity to share Christ right where he was. That experience caused him to write, "Now I want you to know, brethren, that my circumstances have turned out for the greater progress of the gospel, so that my imprisonment in the cause of Christ has become well known throughout the whole praetorian guard and to everyone else, and that most of the brethren, trusting in the Lord because of my imprisonment, have far more courage to speak the word of God without fear" (Phil. 1:12). Adversity and discouragement challenge us, but we can continue in grace and hope to finish the job! What we may see as a mistake or even a disaster, God views as a detour that He uses to fulfill His purpose for us.

Spiritual Attack of Fear

Are you afraid to give your life for Christ's service? Are you uncomfortable to "count the cost"? Sometimes fear attacks and threatens to prevent us from moving forward in our commitment to ministry. There are several fear factors that we may deal with:

1. **Loss of freedom.** You may have thoughts similar to these: "If I go into full-time ministry, I will not be to do what I want to do. I won't be able to have the career I've always desired." Salvation allows you to do whatever God wills. Christ has set you free! Remember, in the first chapter you learned that if you can do anything else and be happy, do it! Freedom comes as you align yourself with God's will. If He has called you to vocational ministry, you will experience freedom within that call.
2. **Loss of finances.** Maybe you are in debt or someone has convinced you that committing your life to Christian service will leave you poor and starving. God will never lead to a place beyond His care and provision. As you are in the preparation stages of ministry, it is wise to be free from debt, but don't use that as an excuse to stall your pursuit of doing

God's will. You may be able to make more money in another career, but you will not be fulfilled or at rest, and spiritual misery is destructive. No one is more miserable than the person who lives by flesh instead of by faith. The person who has a fat bank account but is living out of the will of God is personally bankrupt. Trust God, seek Him first, and He will take care of your needs.

3. **Loss of family relationships.** You may be afraid of what family members may say when told of your commitment to ministry. If you enjoy a close family relationship, you may try to negotiate with God so He'll keep you close in proximity to them. While it's good to love and enjoy family, obedience is much more important than living close to family. To the man who wanted to bury his father before following Christ, Jesus said, ". . . allow the dead to bury their own dead. . ." (Luke 9:59-60). Jesus knew the man was exalting his family over the will of God. You will never be of use in kingdom ministry if living close to family is more important than serving Christ. To those who are married and possibly have children, you are in the middle of changing careers in order to be in vocational ministry. Talking to your spouse and praying together are vital steps in this process. You must work through it as a couple. Pray for your children, talk with them, let them share with you in this transition. Be sensitive, remembering that they are experiencing a change in identity just as you are. Your wife may be working through thoughts such as, "I didn't marry a minister; I don't want to be a minister's wife." These concerns are valid, but don't let family fears hinder you from obeying God's will for your life.

4. **Loss of control over your future.** You may be

wondering what your future will look like as you become a vocational minister. We all experience moments when we feel as though we're looking our future in the face and the unpredictability of it all is scary. I remember the night before I got married, I was hit with the startling realization that I wasn't going to be single anymore. My future as a married man would not look anything like the past. I took a long walk in the neighborhood in the wee hours of the morning, weighing the future. Suddenly a river of peace replaced the storm of anxiety as I thought about how much I loved the girl I would marry and how much she loved me. The thought of losing her far outweighed the fear of losing my single life. The person who loses sight of God's calling because of fear about the future will be miserable. What a privilege to know your future beams brightly as you commit to serve the King of kings in Christian ministry. Keeping your focus on Christ and maintaining a close relationship with Him will ease fear as you realize the incredible privilege of joining Him in His work.

The Spiritual Attack of Unhealthy Relationships

I have seen well-intentioned people become sidetracked and even derailed because of unhealthy friendships. We can again apply I Corinthians 15:33, "'Bad company corrupts good morals.'" As you seek God's will and pursue vocational ministry, understand that you have a vital need for godly friends who will encourage you and pray for you. Ungodly friends will not tell you the truth. They will try to convince you that God's will for you is not ministry, going against what you know to be true for your life. They will even tempt you to abandon your desire to live a holy life.

While you should never stop loving unbelievers and sharing Christ with them, they should not be considered a spiritually reliable support base. As you pursue Christian service, ask God for at least one friend who will challenge you spiritually, build you up, and pray for you consistently.

Another important relationship is marriage. If you are unmarried, choose carefully whom you date. I have been in the ministry long enough to know that a godly spouse is crucial in vocational ministry. It's a good rule to not date anyone you do not intend to marry. This sounds harsh, but innocent and light dating can get serious. Is the person you currently date supportive of your call to ministry? If not, you must end the relationship or suffer disastrous consequences. Trust the Lord in your love relationship. He knows your need for godly friends and a supportive mate. Seek Him and His righteousness, and all of your personal needs will be met from the overabundance of God's love for you.

Spiritual Attack of the Flesh

As believers, we are free from the curse and eternal consequence of sin. However, we still encounter tension between the flesh and the spirit. Paul said in Romans, "For I know that nothing good dwells in me, that is, in my flesh; for the wishing is present in me, but the doing of the good is not. For the good that I wish, I do not do; but I practice the very evil that I do not wish" (7:18-19). Paul, a dynamic Christian and minister of the gospel, freely and publicly confessed his struggle with fleshly nature. Is there something you struggle with that woos you? Is there some potential area of your life that is a weakness, a stronghold? A dear friend and mentor of mine, Dr. C.E. Autrey, has passed on to glory now, but while he was alive, we would sit and talk occasionally. Our "talks" were what I would have envisioned the Apostle Paul and

Timothy might have had. Dr. Autrey, while in his mid-eighties, once looked at me with a stern countenance and warned, "Beware of seductive women, desire for money, and losing your temper." That admonition has always stayed with me. Paul said it like this to Timothy, "Now flee from youthful lusts, and pursue righteousness, faith, love, and peace, with those who call on the Lord from a pure heart" (II Timothy 2:22). The writer of I John relates the same warning: "For all that is in the world, the lust of the flesh, and the lust of the eyes, and the boastful pride of life, is not from the Father, but is from the world" (2:16). Let's take time to look deeper into these traps of the flesh.

- **The lust of the flesh.** Lust is an insatiable desire that could be sexual in nature or it could be any unholy desire that leads to idolatry. Examine your life for a weakness that you need to confess to God. You may need to enlist the help of a mature Christian who would pray with you and help you become accountable as you grow spiritually. A friend of mine once said, "The nature you feed is the one that influences your life." If you feed the flesh and starve the spirit, you will walk under the influence of the flesh. But, if you starve the flesh and feed your spiritual nature, you will walk in the Spirit.
- **The lust of the eyes.** Your eyes take snapshots that are imprinted in the brain and filed away in the heart. Your senses, especially sight, feed your nature. Your eyes can become a gateway into the fleshly nature. Guard them from sinful images, especially pornography, which ensnares in a destructive grip. Be on the alert from seemingly innocent publications and movies that are the product of the world's sensually powerful image-marketing tool.
- **The boastful pride of life.** Pride is the opposite of

humility. It is interested in self-glory instead of self-denial. Pride sneaks in ministry when those who sing, teach, preach or administrate events begin to see themselves as bringing about a spiritual result worthy of the glory that belongs only to God. Humility attracts God; pride pushes Him away (Psalm 138:6; James 4:6). Begin your ministry seeking to serve out of humility. Ego and arrogance drive people away from the cross of Christ more quickly than any other sin. It was pride that kept Satan out of heaven. It was pride that made Adam and Eve weak with sin. Virtually every sin we commit is fueled by the attitude of pride. An effective ministry leader is a humble servant-leader.

Many vocational ministers have left the ministry because of failure due to the fleshly nature. Some have been dishonest; others have shattered their families because of moral failure. When a vocational minister falls because of moral failure, it has a huge ripple effect on the family, the ministry, and the community. It causes hurt feelings and confusion. The minister becomes a stumbling block to weak or immature believers. While fleshly failure has many manifestations, there are four reasons why ministers get to the point of committing sins of an immoral nature: they become emotionally unrested, mentally unchallenged, spiritually unrefreshed, and physically unaccountable. Let's explore each of these.

1. **Emotionally unrested.** Several times in scripture we see Jesus withdraw from a crowd. Mark 1:35 records that Jesus went to a solitary place before daylight. If you read the chapter before verse 35, you see that Jesus endured long days both physically and

emotionally. As a minister loves and cares for people, many situations are emotionally draining more than physically draining. When emotions are spent, they resemble a roller coaster, obscuring thoughts, making problems seem out of proportion, and causing words and actions that were never intended. When this happens, you must learn to withdraw and become emotionally recharged.

2. **Mentally unchallenged.** The mind in neutral is dangerous. It needs to be challenged, mentally exercised just like the body. Stay mentally sharp by reading challenging new material, making yourself aware of what is going on in the world, setting personal goals to read new books and publications. I know a man who succumbed to moral failure because he was unchallenged. His brain functioned in neutral; he stopped researching and studying and his life became predictable. Unfortunately, the challenge he allowed into his life was an adulterous relationship which nearly cost him his marriage and did cost him his ministry. Staying mentally sharp and focused will keep you free from boredom.

3. **Spiritually unrefreshed.** Is it worse to burn out or rust out? The answer is "yes" to both because they both take you "out." As you feed, teach, sing, and spiritually care for people, you need times of spiritual refreshing. Take time to listen to someone at a conference, concert, or retreat setting. The minister who doesn't stay spiritually refreshed becomes parched, resentful, and cold. Schedule a spiritual retreat alone – just you and God – and be quiet and still so He can speak to you. This will energize you and ready you for the demands you face daily.

4. **Physically unaccountable.** Do not neglect your own physical needs. Give your body adequate rest,

exercise, and healthful foods. When I see people pushing themselves to the extreme without eating well or sleeping, I tell them, "Take care of yourself; I need you over the long haul." If you are not getting the right nutrition and you're averaging three hours of sleep a night, you will not enjoy a long, fruitful ministry. When you are exhausted, your people will not enjoy you. There is another principle here. Aside from taking care of yourself, make sure your time is accountable. Someone should know where you are at all times. Teenagers love to be doing things their parents don't know about, a husband can easily get caught up in innocuous activities and forget to tell his wife where he is, ministers can be out and about with no one knowing their whereabouts. This can be dangerous ground if it becomes a habit. I try to keep this simple rule as a pastor: my secretary knows where I am all day; my wife knows where I am all night. If you have tendencies to get away and not tell anyone your location, you are likely to fall into the trap of sin. Being unaccountable for long periods of time can become a playground for temptation. I do not make myself accountable because others don't trust me; I stay accountable because I do not trust myself. Keeping yourself physically cared for and accountable will provide the longevity and integrity needed in ministry.

Several years ago, I was asked to go to South Africa for three weeks to serve on a leadership training team. After our team traveled and trained South African leaders for two and a half weeks, we enjoyed a two-day safari in Kruger Park, the largest national inhabited large-game refuge in the world. The small bus we were traveling in made its way down single lane dirt roads. We saw all kinds of animals and enjoyed the incredible experience of seeing them in their natural habitat instead of in a cage at a zoo.

One afternoon as we were riding, the driver suddenly stopped the bus. We noticed some African deer grazing in a grassy area to our left. A hedgerow stood between the grassy area and the road, acting as a buffer for the deer. The drivers motioned for us to look to the right side of the road. There were two dog-like animals trotting together toward the road. Instinctively, the animals stopped. Their powerful sense of smell told them of the deer nearby. The driver told us these animals were hyenas with a blood-thirsty nature and jaws powerful enough to crush the thigh bone of an adult male. The hyenas sensed there was something on the other side of the hedgerow. We glanced back at the deer on our left and saw a buck raise his mighty head and snort a warning. At once he led the herd safely into the woods. But there was one small fawn grazing so far behind the herd that it never noticed the warning from the leader. This lone fawn did not know the encroaching danger as it grazed carefree, unaware that the rest of its herd had left. We noticed one hyena approaching the rear of the hedgerow and another one strategically walking quietly around the front of the hedgerow. The driver then started the vehicle and drove away from the scene. We all knew that the lone small deer would become a meal for its predators, being no match for the pair of stealthy hunters who sought to devour it.

I have thought of that incident many times through the years. It is a reminder to me and to all of us that we must stay in close fellowship with God and on the alert. Our spiritual attacker waits for us to become exhausted, unrefreshed, and unaccountable. Your spiritual power and strength come from the Lord Jesus. The Holy Spirit indwells you and your wisdom comes from staying in the Word of God.

Maybe you are still wondering, even struggling, with whether God really has called you into ministry. I hope this book has been an encouragement and will help you sort through the many issues you face as you consider your future in serving Christ. If you have moved past the struggle and are sure that God has placed the high calling to Christian ministry on you, I encourage you to take the principles in this book and incorporate them into your life. In the book of Acts, Paul shares his deep concern that he might finish his course and ministry which he received from the Lord. With confidence in the Lord he said, "But I do not consider my life of any account as dear to myself, in order that I may finish my course, and the ministry which I received from the Lord Jesus, to testify solemnly of the gospel of the grace of God" (Acts 20:24). He did finish well, and near the end of his life, he could confidently pen these words: "I have fought the good fight, I have finished the course, I have kept the faith; in the future there is laid up for me the crown of righteousness, which the Lord, the righteous Judge will award to me on that day; and not only to me, but also to all who have loved His appearing" (II Timothy 4:7-8).

Finishing well is as important as the race itself. Many start with good intentions, and may even have a long celebrated run, but don't quite make a successful finish. Stuart Briscoe, a mentor of mine for many years, wrote that in order to stay in ministry and finish well, a minister must have the mind of a scholar, the faith of a child, and the hide of a rhinoceros! Study hard, trust the Lord, and pursue the will of God in the face of opposition. As a minister of the gospel, may you develop a heart after God's own heart and finish well!

Determine *Your* Next Step

Take a few moments to reflect on the main points of Chapter Seven.

- Discouragement and spiritual attack are unavoidable in ministry.
- Cold water comes from many forms:
  1. From loved ones and friends
  2. From personal hardship
  3. From fear
  4. From unhealthy relationships
  5. From the flesh
- You are more vulnerable to discouragement and spiritual attack when you become emotionally unrested, mentally unchallenged, spiritually unrefreshed, and physically unaccountable.
- A major part of your calling is to finish strong!

Now respond to these questions with an open and honest heart:

1. How do you plan to combat spiritual attacks you will encounter in ministry? Write down passages of scripture that will help shield your mind and heart when the attacks come. Commit them to memory.

2. Examine your life for weak areas. How can you protect and strengthen those areas?

3. How do you plan to finish ministry? What are the steps you will take in order to finish well?

4. After having read this book, do you have greater insight and clarity regarding your future? Has the

Lord spoken more directly concerning your role in ministry? Record what He has revealed to you and what you plan to do next in following His lead.

Pond Gap
Ms Pardue's Class
Kathy 909-9040

Printed in the United States
2022 1LVS00001B/673-717